Architects of Aviation

OTHER BOOKS BY MAURICE HOLLAND

INDUSTRIAL TRANSITION OF JAPAN

INDUSTRIAL EXPLORERS *(with H. F. Pringle)*

PROFITABLE PRACTICE IN INDUSTRIAL
RESEARCH *(with others)*

ARCHITECTS OF AVIATION

BY MAURICE HOLLAND
INDUSTRIAL RESEARCH ADVISER
WITH THOMAS M. SMITH
DEPARTMENT OF THE HISTORY OF SCIENCE
UNIVERSITY OF WISCONSIN

DUELL, SLOAN AND PEARCE · NEW YORK

748639

Dedicated to

MY DAD

Whose favorite saying:

"Give 'em the flowers—
while they can still smell them"

*epitomizes the central
theme of this book.*

—Maurice Holland

Contents

Preface

This book is about men. Men of faith and courage whose distinction lies in their proven achievements. Their work put in place the foundation stones of an industrial enterprise which today is building the best military aircraft on earth and is equipping airlines with efficient, safe, and comfortable ships which are the pride of operating staffs and the pleasure of air-minded Mr. and Mrs. America.

Beginning with Jerry Hunsaker, who studied the work of the great French engineer, Eiffel, and learned many of the secrets of the science of aerodynamics from wind measurements taken on that famous world tower, we see the panorama of aviation progress in America unfolding before our eyes as men seek to conquer the skies.

We see the quiet epic of Don Bruner, struggling alone at night with bicycle lamps on his "Jenny" in order that one day the ships of our modern airlines may fly the clock around and make an overnight hop from New York to Los Angeles merely a businessman's "routine trip" to the coast.

We see the stubborn persistence of Bill Stout, who sold aviation to Henry Ford and pioneered in methods of manufacturing metal planes. We see Swede Nelson, whose sure and practical knowledge of airplanes and engines contributed no small part to the success of the U.S. Army planes with open cockpits and water-cooled Liberty engines which made the first round-the-world flight in 1924.

Then there is Major Hoffman, another familiar figure around the hangars at McCook Field when I did my stint there as a test pilot. Hoffman invented "Dummy Joe," a lifelike figure who played Charlie McCarthy to Hoffman's Bergen and was the hero of a thousand jumps before a man alive was allowed to test Hoff's parachutes. I could go on down through the list of familiar names and daring deeds—Charlie Lawrance and Colonel Bane and Captain Stevens and the others—if time and space permitted some personal reminiscences. But this is not my book. Nor is it the book of my old McCook Field associate, Maury Holland.

This is their book—the book of those men who were first, those men most of whose names are barely, if at all, known to the general public. For their exploits have not been written in dramatic headlines. Instead, their great contributions to aviation's progress have lain buried in a set of figures in some battered laboratory notebook or have been gathering dust as crude models in forgotten storerooms. It is indeed time that their achievements be entered plainly in the record for all to see.

Maury tells me that over five years of painstaking research and checking with original sources, combined with the unstinted cooperation of both Army and Navy information services, have gone into this record of the lives and achievements of these architects of aviation.

PREFACE

I have the honor of being an intimate acquaintance of all the pioneers mentioned in the book. Their contributions have been basic. Their names will endure. If this book inspires one young man to adopt a career in the scientific, engineering, or technical fields of aviation—if one potential Hunsaker or Hoffman is uncovered by this story of men who were first in aviation—then the author's time and effort will not have been spent in vain.

—JIMMY DOOLITTLE

Architects of Aviation

Introduction

The process by which progress has been made within historic times . . . is the discovery of new knowledge by each generation and the transmission to the following generation of the accumulated accomplishment of the past— the discovery of new truth and the passing on of old truth.

—*Robert A. Millikan*

One of New York City's favorite, traditional "outdoor sports" is excavation-watching. In all the bustle and tension of metropolitan life there are always those who will pause along their way to watch while other men open up the bowels of the earth with steel-toothed bites of the steam shovel, pour streams of concrete, and swing into place the steel girders that form the skeleton of still another skyscraper.

Through the chattering bedlam of rivet guns on steel they stand undisturbed by the clamor, watching fascinatedly while steelworkers clamber with seeming carelessness on narrow girders high above the street. So do they pay unconscious tribute to the men whose strength and skill force stone and steel to dizzy heights.

Yet, how many of those watchers give so much as a thought to the toilers behind shop and laboratory walls whose work has made possible the modern skyscraper? Do they think at all of research done by metallurgists who use

3

as building blocks of infinite number and complexity the atoms of alloys and steel? Do they picture in their minds the maze of mathematical formulas employed by engineers during countless hours of checking every stress and strain? Do they wonder at the seeming magic of modern miracle-makers who anticipate, with mathematical certainty through models and tests, every condition the full-scale structure will meet in service? No one but a scientist or an engineer could be expected to have a true picture of the infinitely complicated calculations, tests, plans, blueprints, and checks which lie along the road of those who develop and build, from conception to completion.

In the same manner it is too easy for the public mind to take aviation for granted today. Yet both the skyscraper, rooted solidly to the earth and reaching upward toward aviation's roadstead, and the airplane itself drew life at their birth from common sources.

Problems of wind pressure and the resistance of objects to the wind greatly interested Gustave Eiffel, both before and after he built his famous tower in Paris. His researches led him to publish a series of highly technical publications on the force of the wind, and finally a book on the resistance of objects to the air—objects which could as well be cross-sections of a girder in a steel tower as wing struts in an early biplane. Eiffel's book, translated into English by Jerome C. Hunsaker, was instrumental in fostering the study of aerodynamics in America a decade after the Wright brothers first successfully took to the air in 1903.

Since that time the airplane has become a product of

more intensive scientific research than the skyscraper. Aviation is utterly typical of modern, science-aided industry, for today man's flying prowess is laid on a bedrock of pure science. Years ago, in academic quiet far from awestruck spectators, this bedrock was first laid bare, and upon it a research structure began to rise. The cornerstone was placed without ceremony during an occasion that went unrecorded. They who worked in those early years have gone largely unacclaimed and unapplauded.

This book is by no means an attempt to give recognition to every aviation pioneer, or to all the workers in science and technology who have made contributions to aviation. It has been the sincere endeavor here to present, by careful selection and with the polled advice of aviation editors and authorities, twelve of those men whose research laid the groundwork for present-day aviation. Let it be understood that there is here no desire to minimize or depreciate the achievements of the pilots of skill and daring whose flights contributed scientifically as well as dramatically to aviation's progress. As long as men have been able to produce a machine that would fly there have been other stout-hearted men who risk their lives to fly them, and it cannot be said that one was the more valuable than the other. But the great pilots, by the dramatic nature of their undertakings, have achieved some public recognition and appreciation. We have made it our task to present the stories of those other men who did so much to make the flights possible, men who were first. While many of them were themselves fliers, most of their work for aviation was done with slide rule rather than joystick. Without them man might still be trusting his life to rickety crates, and engines might still be the hit-or-miss, undependable contraptions which floundered on wings in the wind in earlier days.

These, then, are representative of the men who made possible the science of aviation in America. Aviation being the prodigy that it is, many of them are still alive. Some are still contributing to aviation's progress. Most of them have lived to see their dreams and prophecies come true. Indeed, the expectations of many have been far exceeded by the rapid advances of aeronautics. And though each year brings new engineers, designers, and builders of aircraft, all constantly working to improve practical aviation or its theoretical bases of scientific understanding, these pioneers whose stories follow play unique roles in the history of American aeronautical science. The impress of their footprints in aviation's yesterday has made possible the wing-prints in the skies today.

Chapter 1

MAN OF MANY FIRSTS

Jerome C. Hunsaker

When the cornerstone of aviation technology is eventually opened on some future historic occasion, we will find enclosed in it a copy of Gustave Eiffel's book *Resistance of the Air and Aviation*. A single volume, a summary of one man's lifework in science, provided the basis for the technology of present-day aeronautical engineering as inaugurated and developed in America by Jerome C. Hunsaker.

Before this, all aeronautical developments had been obtained by empirical experiments like the great "first" of the Wrights at Kitty Hawk. Hunsaker, truly the man of many firsts, established aeronautics in America as a science; he stands as a striking example of the quiet, thinking men whose work brought aviation from a daredevil's sporting gamble with death to an established, science-aided, modern transport industry.

Hunsaker the man is overshadowed by his achievements.

7

Every incident of aeronautics today follows along paths laid down in Hunsaker's first American course in aeronautical engineering. Wind tunnels follow the first one in America, designed by him at Massachusetts Institute of Technology; the first transatlantic flights were in the NC's of Hunsaker's design and construction; his was the first American rigid airship, the ill-fated "Shenandoah." Today's network of radio communications, bringing weather reports that make possible commercial airlines, rests upon the foundation laid by Jerome Hunsaker in his experiments with the first "flying laboratory" of Bell Telephone Laboratories. He was the operating executive of the first projected American commercial air transport line which planned to use Zeppelin-type equipment. He was the first President of the American Institute for the Aeronautical Sciences, the foremost scientific institution of areonautics in America, patterned after the distinguished Royal Aeronautical Society of Great Britain.

The skyscraper and the airplane, two of the most striking visible exponents of modern civilization, were born of common origins. Gustave Eiffel, rearing his steel tower skyward beside the Seine, can scarcely have realized how much the graceful embodiment of his fancy was to give lifeblood to the science of aviation. Permitting himself no great mass of brick or stone or concrete to flout the winds of heaven, Eiffel had to calculate with accuracy the wind pressures his slender spider web of steel must carry and the stresses it must stand. The problems involved elaborate experiments with wind velocity and intricate calculations of the proposed tower's stability under varying weather conditions. From this and later research, Eiffel developed a technique of experimental aerodynamics which was later set forth in a book that has become a pioneer classic in the study of aeronautics.

Meanwhile, a boy in Saginaw, Michigan, who had never heard of Eiffel's name was dreaming of a career at sea. Jerome Hunsaker's father, W. J. Hunsaker, was a newspaper publisher actively interested in Michigan's Republican politics. The local Congressman was "Sugar Beet" Joe Fordney, who had appointed a boy to the Naval Academy at Annapolis. Young Hunsaker's opportunity came when the appointee failed in his entrance examinations and Hunsaker was offered the next appointment in 1904.

Four years of intensive study and drill at Annapolis disciplined him mentally and hardened him physically. He found that the work was comparatively easy for him, and he led his class in the competitive examination. It was the tradition for two or three of the best students to apply for transfer to the Naval Construction Corps and Hunsaker made his application. While Hunsaker, Jr. was doing service at sea the first year after his graduation, Hunsaker, Sr. went trout fishing with his friend Truman Newberry of Detroit, then Secretary of the Navy. As a result of their conversation a check-up demonstrated that young Hunsaker's definite pioneering bent and creative sense were recognized by his instructors, so Newberry ordered him to report to Massachusetts Institute of Technology for graduate study prior to his transfer to the Construction

Corps. Ordinarily he should have spent two years at sea, instead of one, after graduation.

But the designing of super-dreadnoughts did not entirely satisfy young Hunsaker. He felt the weight of tradition rather than its inspiration; the science of warship building had settled along lines too well established to offer the challenge which was essential to a man fired with imagination and inspired by scientific curiosity. Shortly before his appointment to Massachusetts Institute of Technology, the Wrights had made their epoch-making flight at Kitty Hawk, stirring the imagination of the whole world. The effect upon Hunsaker, already committed to a scientific career in the Navy, was compelling. About the time of his graduation in 1912 with the degree of Master of Science in naval architecture, the first Squantum aviation meet was held and Earle Ovington flew a French Bleriot machine around Boston Harbor. There was great interest, particularly at the Institute, in why these planes could fly and Professor C. H. Peabody suggested that Hunsaker try to find out. He searched out and absorbed the writings of Langley, Lilienthal, Chanute, Mouillard, and the then current work of Eiffel on the wind tunnel. The latter, particularly, seemed to furnish an engineering basis for design which would replace the art of the inventor's often empirical approach.

After his graduation in the summer of 1912, Hunsaker and his wife worked on a translation of Eiffel's book and obtained the author's permission to publish it. Hunsaker had found several mistakes in Eiffel's calculations, and the

French scientist was pleased by this evidence of the young American's care and zeal. No publisher could see any possible market for so specialized a work, but by this time Hunsaker's interest had been definitely committed to aeronautical science and his enthusiasm for the work was so great that he agreed to furnish the plates for the book at his own expense. Accordingly, Houghton Mifflin of Boston and Constable of London agreed to handle it, and the book was published in 1913, selling well to schools and designers. The expense of the plates was quickly returned to the author, and he made something over the amount of his gamble.

While Hunsaker was translating Eiffel's treatise, his work was drawn to the attention of the President of Massachusetts Institute of Technology, Doctor Richard Maclaurin. In the spring of 1913 Maclaurin asked the Navy to assign Hunsaker to M. I. T. to inaugurate a course in aeronautical engineering. Being assigned at that time to the Boston Navy Yard as Assistant Shop Superintendent, a job that he found not particularly congenial, Hunsaker welcomed the opportunity. Almost immediately he was sent abroad, by Maclaurin's arrangement, to learn about research methods used in France, England, and Germany. He was armed with letters to Maclaurin's academic friends as well as with introductions from Doctor Charles D. Walcott of the Smithsonian Institution.

By this time the die was cast. Jerome C. Hunsaker was embarked upon an adventure into the unknown, not upon oceans familiar to the Navy but upon the almost uncharted seas of aeronautical science. His first major contribution had been making the Eiffel classic work available to students. (It is still in service as a reference book.) While abroad, Hunsaker was welcomed to Eiffel's famous laboratories at Auteuil, near Paris. At this time Eiffel was nearly blind, but each afternoon he came to the laboratory and had his assistants Rith and Laprestle read to him the data obtained that day and describe the nature of the curves they had obtained by plotting the data. Eiffel cross-examined them on methods used and discussed the significance of the results. To Hunsaker it was both an inspiration and a liberal education to be intimately associated with a truly great engineer and to observe him in the exercise of his judgment after critical examination of the day's experiments. Eiffel never lost sight of his objective or of the precision of measurements involved in the investigations.

Frequently Eiffel was joined for discussion of aerodynamic problems by another old man and great engineer, Stephane Drzewiecki, who lived nearby and who was the author of the blade-element theory of propeller design, which had not then been accepted by designers for the powerful method it later became.

Aeronautical science in Europe was, at that time, considerably in advance of America, and Hunsaker had set out to absorb all that he could carry of Europe's knowledge. From France he went on to England, where he was received with great kindliness by Sir Richard Glazebrook, then Director of the National Physical Laboratory, a British organization somewhat similar to the American Bureau of Standards. Sir Richard put him up at Bushy House and, after entertaining him at lunch, turned him over to Dr. T. E. Stanton and Dr. Leonard Bairstow, the most distinguished aerodynamics team of that time. He was taken on as an assistant to read a velocity gauge which indicated the air speed in the wind tunnel. Hunsaker is frank to admit today that it was several days before he quite understood just what he was doing or why. But it was stimulating to be part of a group of enthusiastic young men who were working on problems of an entirely new field of science. In that day almost any question about aerodynamics led to a new problem. It was principally during his stay in England that Hunsaker absorbed the experience enabling him later to build the first American wind tunnel at M. I. T. The American tunnel was an improvement on the design of the one he had worked on at Teddington, England.

There was no rumor of war at that time. An American enthusiast was not treated as a spy but more as a sportsman who had come to join in the game to help as he could until he, too, could learn to play. Through the Military Attaché in London, Major George O. Squier (later to become Chief of the Army Air Service), he met the leaders of the British Aeronautical Academy, among whom at the flying field at Hendon was a young engineer named Handley Page, who seemed to have revolutionary ideas. Major Baden-Powell, then a balloonist, later head of the Boy Scouts, was another of Hunsaker's early English acquaintances.

Hunsaker's next stop was in Germany. There, thanks to Dr. Albert F. Zahm, who had been sent over by the Smithsonian, many scientific circles were opened up for the young American, though there was still a closed iron ring around military aeronautics. He visited Göttingen, but the Zeppelin works were not open to overseas visitors. They did arrange to book passage as tourists for a ride over Berlin on the Zeppelin that was doing propaganda flights to popularize the Zeppelin building programs. Dr. Zahm insisted upon taking a bottle of champagne aloft and drinking a toast to the palace of the Kaiser. Just as they passed over the roof, Zahm tossed a glassful out—"so that I can tell about this impudence to my grandchildren or yours, if ever there be any," he laughed.

At the airport at Johannesthal, Hunsaker met a young Dutchman named Anthony Fokker, who was building an experimental monoplane in a hangar there. He expected to sell it to the German Army, but since he had not yet done so there was no secret about it. It did not look like a very impressive craft, compared with the later, trim, fighting Taube and the swift, diving Albatross, but it really was clean in design, simple in construction, and a joy to the pilot because of its easy control.

Bringing with him the digested data and experiences of his European trip, Hunsaker returned to M. I. T. in 1914. With President Maclaurin's authorization, he organized a course of studies leading to a Master of Science degree in aeronautical engineering, thus becoming the first instructor in the first course of its kind in America. His first student was Alexander Klemin, who later followed in Hunsaker's footsteps as an instructor. Other early students, who were later figures in American aviation, were V. E. Clark and Lieutenants B. Q. Jones and H. W. Harms of the Army. The Navy ordered all student officers at M. I. T. to take the new aeronautics course in addition to naval construction and architecture. About this time, too, Donald W. Douglas, who was later to achieve fame, first as chief designer of the Glenn Martin Company and later as a leading aircraft designer and constructor, had just graduated from a mechanical engineering course. Douglas became Hunsaker's assistant in setting up the wind tunnel and initiating aerodynamic research.

The wind tunnel was, and is, the heart of aeronautical research, and a word on its function may be of value. In naval architecture, a designer has a small model of his ship towed in an experimental model basin. From the resistance of the model he can estimate the resistance of his ship and so estimate precisely its speed for a given power.

For purposes of airplane or airship design it is possible to tow models in the air in a somewhat similar manner. However, in aeronautics the problem is extremely complex. In flight, motion is possible along the *three axes* in space (wingtip to tip, nose to tail, pilot's transparent enclosure to cockpit floor), as well as by *rotation* about any of them. Therefore, accepting that aerodynamic forces depend upon the relative motion of the air and the subject under test, it is immaterial whether the object be towed in still air at a given velocity or held stationary in a uniform current of air of the same velocity. This use of an artificially generated wind is the wind tunnel method which had come into general use abroad, and which it was Hunsaker's first task to establish at M. I. T.

The tunnel he built at Boston was in accordance with the plans of the one he had worked on in England, with the exception of several changes of an engineering nature. These changes were introduced to obtain a more economical use of power and gave an increase of maximum wind speed from thirty-four to forty miles per hour.

The wind tunnel proper was a trunk sixteen feet square and sixty-three feet in length. Air was drawn through an entrance nozzle and blown through the tunnel by an airplane propeller powered by a ten-horsepower motor. The airplane models, wind sections, etc. were mounted in the middle of the tunnel on the arm of a delicate balance which had been ordered from England, and which gave an accurate measurement of various factors of resistance. The motor and propeller unit was mounted in concrete and set independently of the tunnel structure so that no vibration was transmitted. Any wind speed between three and forty miles per hour could be produced.

On the basis of his research at M. I. T. on the dynamic stability of airplanes Hunsaker was awarded, by the Institute, the degree Doctor of Science in 1916; a degree which, conferred at M. I. T., represents one of the ultimate accolades in engineering science.

Shortly after, Lieutenant-Instructor Hunsaker was called from Boston and the quiet calm of his academic research and teaching duties to Washington to head the newly created Aircraft Division in the Construction Department of the Navy.

A single draftsman and a secretary completed the personnel, and it was from these small beginnings that an immense organization was to develop rapidly under the forced draft of wartime emergency.

David W. Taylor, Chief Constructor of the Navy, encouraged Hunsaker to develop this division and gave him broad powers which eventually developed into responsibility for all naval aircraft, including design, construction, and procurement during the war period. But before we entered the war the bogey of long-range cruising submarines was raised with the startling appearance of the "Deutschland" on the Atlantic seaboard. The first problem to be met was the protection of our Eastern coast against such sea wolves. Lieutenant John Towers was sent abroad by the Navy to investigate the torpedoing of an American vessel in the war zone. While in England Towers flew one of the British airships especially designed for duty against the submarine and when he returned his observations aided Hunsaker to develop the series of non-rigid airships later known as blimps.

During the years of American participation in the war, 1917–19, Hunsaker was in charge of naval aircraft design, construction, and procurement, and developed, with the co-operation of the Navy and the Curtiss Company, a series of flying boats, both single- and multi-motored, and powered by Liberty engines. By speeding up production of material, the United States shipped abroad several hundred flying boats to give protection to American transports and to patrol the principal seaports. At the end of one year nearly a thousand of these American-designed and -built flying boats had been dispatched to France. Hunsaker was paying his debt to Eiffel with interest. There had been a shortage of planes, but so well had the lusty Aircraft Division done its work that the naval aircraft program caught up with the overseas demand. Pilots were not being trained fast enough to take over the new equipment. Orders came from France to hold up further shipments of aircraft.

Perhaps one of Jerome Hunsaker's greatest achievements was the development of the "NC" (Navy-Curtiss) flying boats. During the summer of 1918 the problem of shipping equipment and material to France became acute, and gave promise of becoming even worse. The Service of Supply, anticipating the possibility of the war's lasting several years more, desired to design and build a flying boat that might cross the Atlantic to the war zone under its own power. After a conference of high naval officials in Washington, the problem was passed to Hunsaker in the form of a memorandum from Admiral D. W. Taylor requesting construction of a flying boat with greater size and range than had ever before been thought possible. The development work on this problem eventually led Lieutenant Commander Towers and his fellow officers Reid and Ballinger into the epoch-making flight of the NC boats in the first organized air expedition across the Atlantic.

Three NC boats started from Newfoundland in May 1919, two were left at the Azores, but the NC-4 under command of Commander A. C. Read continued on to Lisbon and Plymouth, making the first crossing of the Atlantic by aircraft of any type.

In the lighter-than-air field Hunsaker was a pioneer in America. As early as 1917 he had designed the first practical American airship. He followed this by the construction of a series of lighter-than-air craft during the war. After the Armistice, while attached to the staff of Admiral Sims as an expert adviser, Hunsaker was able to pursue his investigations of lighter-than-air craft in Germany and to inspect the great Zeppelins which had been so successfully used against the Allies during the war. He also took advantage of this opportunity to observe the progress which Germany had made with flying boats. During this tour of duty in Europe he was signally honored by an invitation to deliver the Wilbur Wright memorial address before the Royal Aeronautical Society of Great Britain. He was made an Honorary Fellow of that Society, the first foreigner and only American to be selected for that distinction.

Returning to America, Hunsaker was called upon to make use of his observations of foreign lighter-than-air construction and was charged with the responsibility of designing the first Zeppelin-type craft which the United States Government undertook to construct. The British were also at work on the dirigible, which about this time had come to be looked upon as the future long-distance aircraft. Thus work came to be started on the "Shenandoah," the first American rigid airship, which after two years' service was wrecked in a storm. Because of the use of helium, a large part of her crew was saved to give a detailed account of what had happened. The ship had evidently not been strong enough for the violence and rapid change of American weather conditions. Its specifications had been deduced through extensive research from the plans of the German Zeppelin L-49 brought down in France during the war, and the "Shenandoah" had been made somewhat stronger than the L-49 in view of the fact that the ship would have to be operated by a comparatively unskilled crew. This tragic experience indicated the need for more extensive radio meteorological reports, trained operators, and greater strength in basic design.

In 1921 the Naval Bureau of Aeronautics was organized and the Airship Division of the Bureau of Construction and Repair transferred to it, Hunsaker becoming Chief of the Materiel Division. His duties remained as before except that engineers for naval aircraft were added. Here Hunsaker found, in the late Admiral W. A. Moffat, an enthusiastic advocate of progress. There was opportunity quickly to realize practical results in the great accumulation of research and experimental data obtained during the war. During the early 1920's Hunsaker divided his attention between the development of airplanes and lighter-than-air craft. His contributions included special features of postwar airplane carriers to permit airplane launching and landing, launching boats, arresting gear for deck landings on aircraft carriers, and the air-cooled radial engine (with Charles L. Lawrance). The winning of the Pulitzer and Schneider Cups and the establishment of a world speed record was another triumph for Hunsaker. The light ship-to-shore plane (with Curtiss and Vought), the torpedo plane, and very substantial improvement of patrol airships and flying boats are milestones along the path of aviation progress which Hunsaker had a hand in laying.

In 1922 Hunsaker recognized the significance of the Handley Page slotted wing and, after wind tunnel experiments, secured the license for its use by the United States Government. The following year he was appointed a member of the National Advisory Committee for Aeronautics and was made Assistant Naval Attaché at London, with advisory duties in which his extensive technical knowledge of aircraft was used on the staffs of the American Embassies at Paris, Berlin, Rome, and the Hague.

Through the gloomy postwar period of deflation, with the sudden reduction of government needs for aircraft, the aviation industry was in a bad way. Hunsaker's pioneering vision of the problems which confronted the industry prompted him to sponsor a farsighted policy. Feeling that the aeronautical designer furnished the lifeblood of the aviation industry, Hunsaker used his influence to keep technology alive in the commercial field. As we had learned to our cost, it was an excellent policy to keep essential industries going in peacetime for possible emergencies. Aviation had demonstrated its importance in wartime, so as a form of encouragement to a lagging industry, the Navy under Hunsaker's urging entered a seaplane team as a contestant in the Schneider Cup Races in which this country had not previously competed. Rittenhouse, piloting for the

United States, broke the speed record by more than fifty miles an hour.

The impression on the general public, however, was transitory in those pre-Lindbergh days. The flight across the Atlantic by the Navy NC boats, and even the more spectacular world-girdling flight of the Army fliers, had little effect in lifting the industry out of the doldrums. In contrast to the later splendid achievements of individuals, these flights were the achievements of organizations—the Navy or the Army—and the public may not have been psychologically geared to receive as heroes the conquerors of the Atlantic in uniforms. It is hard to dramatize an organization.

Faced by a period of stagnation in naval aircraft development, Hunsaker was induced to set aside his brilliant record of technical achievement in the Navy and embark on a commercial career. The Bell Telephone Laboratories, central research organization of our largest telephone system, had decided to make a survey of the possibilities of communications in the aviation industry when, as, and if it arrived.

Always more the scientist than the militarist, Hunsaker found the lure of untried fields in aviation communication too strong to resist. He tackled the problem of fitting communication into the future picture of aviation. There was, too, the additional incentive of the memory of the ill-fated "Shenandoah," which had carried his friends to death and his designs to destruction. Believing as he did that American dirigible failures had been due in great measure to inadequate weather reports, he arranged for the operation of a model meteorological service for a short airline between San Francisco and Los Angeles. At the same time, he arranged to install on other airways a demonstration telephone-typewriter or ticker service, using the long lines of the American Telephone and Telegraph Company. The last and perhaps most important development was a compact and accurate radio-telephone transmitter and receiver for the airplane itself, installed in such a way as to eliminate both ignition interference and mechanical noise. Eventually this combination of wire service, radio service, and meteorological service, substantially as conceived by Hunsaker, was adopted as the standard system of our airways.

With the aerial communication work of the Bell Laboratories well advanced, and the larger problems well on their way toward solution, Hunsaker reluctantly resigned from this interesting interlude in his career and returned to his earlier enthusiasm. Wartime animosities were forgotten and patents were once more internationally respected. The United States Government had entered into negotiations with the Goodyear Company, which had taken over the Zeppelin patents from manufacturers in this country. Scientific exploration in the development of airships again loomed on Hunsaker's horizon.

Eckener had not yet pointed the way toward an amazing future for this type of aircraft by his trip around the world. Giant dirigibles had not spanned continents and crossed the seven seas in experimental operations. Hunsaker was in his element, but he had a battle on his hands. Not only did the natural elements conspire against his new medium of expression, but a series of unfortunate accidents to dirigibles shook the confidence of aeronautical experts and the public. The British Admiralty at about this time publicly announced the abandonment of its military dirigible program. Yet postwar experience in Germany proved that successful commercial operation of dirigibles on passenger and express lines was possible. These German operations held out encouragement that there was a place in the aviation scheme of things for this type of craft, despite the fact that the Germans then seemed to be the only nationals who could design, construct, and operate airships successfully.

Officials of the Goodyear Company saw their opportunity and agreed that one way out was to import lighter-than-air experience from Germany. So they secured both American manufacturing rights and technical assistance from the Zeppelin Company in Germany. Shortly after, the Goodyear Zeppelin Company was established, and contracts were placed with it for building two Zeppelin-type ships for the government. A later development was the organization of the Pacific Zeppelin Transport Company, with Hunsaker as President.

As in the early days of Hunsaker's instructorship at M. I. T., so again the technology of Europe was imported into the great plant established at Akron, Ohio, where the largest dirigible hangar and construction shed in the world were built.

The "Akron" and "Macon" were designed with the aid

24

of the experienced engineers brought from the German Zeppelin Company, strength factors were very greatly increased, yet the "Shenandoah's" experience was repeated. After about a year's successful service the "Akron" was caught in a violent storm while flying at a very low altitude and struck the surface of the sea. The "Macon" had structural trouble with her tail surfaces which was not adequately repaired because the danger was not realized. Later she broke her tail by failure of this structure and was lost. Hunsaker feels that, while the Navy's airship experience was as discouraging as the Germans' was successful, the two factors of weather reports and training of operating personnel, after the manner in which the Germans were thoroughly trained, would solve our dirigible problems.

When the government refused to continue its airship program, Hunsaker finally returned to his old love, the quiet academic calm of a university laboratory. Back at the scene of his early achievements, Hunsaker became head of the Department of Mechanical Engineering at Massachusetts Institute of Technology. There aeronautic engineering at the Institute continued to be carried on as new men and ideas joined the march of aviation progress.

Chapter 2

MASTER OF McCOOK

Thurman H. Bane

McCook Field, at Dayton, Ohio, has been called "the crucible of aviation technology." During and immediately after World War I, in that period of American aviation which eventually brought the United States world leadership in aviation technology, it was the McCook Field group, more than any other single organization, that made the greatest contributions to aeronautical knowledge and practice. And, in the postwar period of commercial aviation's expansion, it was upon McCook's former personnel that private industry drew.

At McCook Field Captain Stevens experimented and perfected aerial photography, Major Hoffman developed the parachute, lifesaver of the air, and Lieutenant Bruner pioneered in night flying experiments that laid the groundwork for the present round-the-clock flight routine. At McCook, Alexander Klemin as a sergeant worked out principles of design and sand-testing that saved countless lives, and Charles Lawrance perfected the Wright Whirlwind engine which was to be for a time the foremost air-cooled power plant in the world. Countless others, many whose names are not marked by fame, toiled at McCook Field that aviation might grow, and in growing, become safer and better. Men of varying temperaments and abilities, drawn from many walks of life, they worked with a co-ordinated unanimity of spirit which was remarkable. And this was in so small measure a tribute to their Commander, Colonel Thurman H. Bane.

Back in 1915, Lieutenant Thurman H. Bane, United States Cavalry, patrolling the Mexican Border, first resolved to enter the Air Service. Bane, born in 1879 and a graduate of West Point in 1907, looked the typical Regular Army man. Neat clipped mustache, beaked aquiline nose, and firm jaw with jutting, fighter's chin were balanced by a high impressive forehead. And while he was fond of the cavalry, on that day in 1915 he looked up from the hard seat of a McClellan saddle and watched, inspired by the flight of Army planes droning in massed formation over-head. There—in the air—was freedom from the grind of cavalry patrol over interminable stretches of flat country covered with mesquite, cactus, and alkali dust. The comparative futility of cavalry scouting was obvious to Bane when he compared it with these winged scouts that could traverse in one hour a distance it would take a troop three days to cross. Perhaps, too, he saw a new freedom and romance in the air; and he may have dreamed of the place aeronautics would some day make in the world, a place he would help establish.

The airplane in America was maturing slowly while young Bane was doing his border patrol work along the Rio Grande. In 1912, when Bane was assigned to the Ordnance Department, an airplane ride was still considered the height of daring, which, in truth, it very nearly was. And it was during the next three years, while he was studying ballistics at Sandy Hook and equipment manufacture at Rock Island Arsenal, that aircraft made those first strides which prepared it for its eventual destiny in the First World War: supplanting the cavalry as the "eyes" of the Army.

After his second service in the cavalry, Bane transferred to the Signal Corps late in 1916 and was sent to North Island for training at the flying school there. Our Army Air Service was embryonic compared to that of most of the larger European powers, who were devoting much money and effort to building aircraft and training men to fly them. In 1909 Wilbur Wright had given the first flight instruction to Army officers at College Park, Maryland, forming the first Army Air squadron. In 1911 Glenn Curtiss invited the Secretary of War and the Secretary of the Navy to send one or more Army and Navy officers to him for instruction in aeronautics. This was offered without charge, since the government had no money appropriation for aviation work. San Diego, California, was selected as the site of the training grounds because of its even climate, and Glenn Curtiss began instruction of a few Army and Navy officers there at North Island. Not until March of 1911 did the first Naval Appropriations Act provide $25,000 for aeronautics and mark the United States as the first country to establish Naval Aviation.

From the training school at North Island, Bane emerged with the wings of Junior Military Aviator. His first ambition was realized. He could fly.

War, meanwhile, was raging in Europe. Bane was alert to the possibilities of an Army air arm, but he saw, too, that American aviation could not hope to advance any more rapidly than its theoretical knowledge and technology permitted. The course in aeronautical engineering at Massachusetts Institute of Technology, inaugurated by Jerome C. Hunsaker, was the foremost and perhaps only comprehensive training course of its kind in America. Hunsaker had been succeeded by Alex Klemin, who at that time was collaborating with T. H. Huff on a series of articles in *Aviation* magazine on aerodynamics, the first comprehensive and exhaustive course of its kind in English. Bane applied himself assiduously to the study of these articles, boned up on the mathematics he had used in his ordnance studies, and bought every book and publication available on the technique and engineering of aviation.

From his extensive studies, and using the series of articles by Klemin and Huff as a foundation, Bane laid out a course in aerodynamics and design which was enthusiastically adopted and he was commissioned to teach it to the flying personnel at North Island. It was something of a tribute to his application and grasp of aeronautics that, within a year of his entering the Air Service, he was an instructor in aeronautical engineering; this without benefit of formal training at an engineering school.

Bane was wholly absorbed in his work. The prestige of military preferment was of secondary importance to him. Nevertheless, his outstanding contributions brought swift recognition and, when the United States was drawn into the war, he was placed at the head of the technical section of the Bureau of Military Aeronautics in Washington, D. C. Here was a position that carried a heavy responsibility. Each of our Allies was intent on having the U. S. Government adopt its own type of plane for our airmen in France. French, British, and Italian missions each extolled the virtues of their particular designs; instances of their respective victories at the front were offered as evidence of superiority under service conditions; pressures were brought to bear and the whole scene resolved into a gigantic maelstrom of national super-salesmanship.

"We had no experience at the front at that time," Bane said of this era, "and we had to take their word. It is therefore not remarkable that our policy was a vacillating one; first one type of plane was employed, then another. It *is* remarkable that we did so well under the circumstances." And it was upon Thurman H. Bane that the responsibility fell of deciding ultimate policies, of co-ordinating the various conflicting claims and offers into a workable air policy, at the same time that he kept national antagonisms at bay.

It is a notable commentary on Bane's wartime service that, after the Armistice, in 1919, he was given command of McCook Field at Dayton.

During and shortly after the war Dayton, Ohio, was the heart of aviation technology in America. At Wilbur Wright Field, Dayton, was the testing department of the Bureau of Military Aeronautics under the command of Major B. Q. Jones. Ten miles away, on the other side of the city, was the Bureau of Aircraft Production under the direction of Colonel William Potter (who was later to become Chairman of the Board of the Guaranty Trust Company). During the war the B. A. P., or Bureau of Aircraft Production, was responsible for the design and construction of military aircraft and the assembly of material, operating with the services of such industrial stars as Jesse Vincent of Packard and Colonel Hall—co-designers of the Liberty engine, Colonel Marmon of Indianapolis, C. F. Kettering, and Colonel E. A. Deeds—all drawn from the automobile industry, which was experienced in production problems similar to those involving the building of military airplanes in quantity. They turned out the famous D. H. planes, attaining enviable records in mass production.

The Bureau of Military Aeronautics (the B. M. A.) at Wright Field formulated the requirements, wrote the specifications, and accepted or rejected the product of the B. A. P. Major B. Q. Jones was himself chief test pilot; here, too, were the tacticians and military authorities of all sorts, putting the results of aircraft production through grueling tests before accepting them for service.

Colonel Bane was brought from Washington and commissioned to consolidate the work of these two organizations—the B. A. P. and the B. M. A.—on a permanent, peacetime basis, and in January of 1919 he took over McCook Field, Dayton, and merged the facilities and personnel of the two units. There were nineteen sections and seventy-five branches to be co-ordinated into a smooth-running machine. Of the 2300 officers and civilians employed at McCook four hundred were scientists, engineers, and technicians. No impresario was ever faced with such a galaxy of temperament, with such a vastly differing group of personalities. That Bane was able to organize the whole into an efficient and harmonious group with a minimum of friction is in itself an achievement of distinction.

But Bane knew his men. His understanding of the human element and his reputation as a square-shooter stood him in good stead. From the "greasenecks" in the hangars to the ranking section chiefs who comprised his staff no one worked for Bane—everyone worked *with* him.

To achieve this took more than mere executive ability. Bane presented the rarity of a Regular Army man who could, for results, forget the formal trumpery of rank and title. He realized that here was a tremendous job to be done by officers, enlisted men, and civilians alike. Results would be best realized by utilizing the various abilities, regardless of the gold braid the men wore. To young officers, and sometimes older men in the service, who were inclined to place a bit too much emphasis on their bars or oak leaves, Colonel Bane would say:

"Gentlemen, when you pass through that gate under the sign reading 'Engineering Division, Army Air Service,' you leave your rank outside. Here we are all students of aeronautical science, and there's more than one shavetail at the field who has more practical knowledge of aircraft design and construction than any high-ranking officer in the service."

It was an attitude that might have been natural to a civilian; it was unusual from an Army commander. Yet it was the one form of approach that got results. Colonel Bane looked upon McCook as the test tube in the laboratory development of air equipment, not as an Army post. He had the vision to see that, unlike routine Army jobs, here was one in which not the collar insignia but what was above the collar counted, and he rated his men by their ability to work with others in the development of faster, better, and more efficient aircraft. By this standard they were advanced. All else was subordinated.

A thousand and one research and development problems were under way simultaneously at McCook. Everything in Army aircraft and its accessories was being studied, from such diverse projects as armored pursuit and ground attack planes to the problem of making a tiny steel needle that would replace one with a sapphire bearing in a delicate instrument; from bomb racks that would carry a thousand-pound bomb to a safety parachute that would carry a man. Effects of sun and exposure on paint, varnish, and wing dope were studied; a concrete pit was built to test propeller blades to destruction, and through it all Bane had to fight a constant battle with higher authority to keep research and development in the important position they deserved.

His first problem was to consolidate and organize the

multitudinous activities of the field, a job that, it soon became apparent, called for more than routine Army organization. Here was an Army post doing the job of a huge research laboratory, and Bane realized that the methods of commercial industry would have to be called upon for efficient organization. He called a meeting of his nineteen section chiefs one morning and outlined his policy.

"Gentlemen," he said, "we are going to form an Industrial Engineering Branch to co-ordinate the activities of McCook Field. You, Holland," he indicated the author, whose pre-Army experience qualified him for the job, "have done a lot of work in private industry gearing industry to production. I want you to go to the library—get all the books and data you need to organize the Industrial Engineering Branch, and we'll lay out a program. Study everything and everybody . . . myself included . . . and find out what cogs are slipping. I don't care who it hits—our problem is production and we've got to lick it."

A survey of Bane's own activities was made, and it was revealed that, of the nineteen section chiefs, four had seen him in one month for conferences; the same four also consistently called upon his time more than any of the others. The conclusions were laid before him: there were four weak sections that *he* was literally running, using valuable time and effort that should have been spread over the entire nineteen.

Bane looked at the figures. "Hmm," he said. "One of those four is a former classmate of mine. I thought he had something on the ball." He looked at the unalterable facts before him again. "But I was wrong." He fired the four and put the sections in more efficient hands.

As the Industrial Engineering Branch began to operate it proved its own efficiency. Gadgets, charts, tables, and figures found their way to his desk, telling their own story of the progress of the work at hand, and periodically Bane called in the staff and raised hell, to use his own words. Yet they loved him for it because the axe never fell on the wrong neck. The framework of organization never became an elaborate end in itself, but remained the means to efficient production. Nor were the officers troubled by the petty annoyances of discipline. Tunics could be undone, boots unshined, and no military martinet brought it curtly to attention. A bewildering variety of costume made any distinction between Army and civilian members of the field almost impossible. Some of the officers worked in knickers and golf hose, others in overalls or slacks. On at least one occasion, when General Pershing was to review the personnel of McCook Field, there was a wild and frantic scurrying before the Army men could find enough uniforms and articles of equipment to present a military appearance.

In those early postwar years Bane's patience and energy underwent severe trials. His problems were not limited merely to running McCook Field and winning his goal of developing faster, better, and more efficient aircraft and equipment. He was forced to wage continuous warfare with higher authority to keep this work in the foreground. Now that the emergency of war had passed there was the increasing tendency in Washington to let aeronautical work slip back to its prewar basis. Even greater was his problem of maintaining the morale of his staff in the face of appropriation cuts and poor pay; this in the face of constantly enlarging opportunities in outside industry. For by this time commercial production in private industry had begun on an unprecedented scale, technicians were in growing demand, and the Army offered only meager compensation. Too, the expanding aeronautical industry, staffed with high-salaried experts, took an attitude of paternalism toward the research work of the Army Air Service. No opportunity was overlooked by private industry in its attempt to lift this work from government hands.

"Eventually," they said, in effect, "the government will come to us for planes. Therefore the money spent in research might better be spent by those companies which are going to produce the future planes."

But in those early postwar days, when the industry was experiencing its first growing pains, Bane knew that the trial-and-error method would not suffice. In the face of administrative economy programs and postwar antipathy, he fought for every appropriation to carry on research.

He fought, too, an army of inventive cranks. It seemed that everyone in the world had "just what the Air Corps needs." They came to Bane with their ideas, and he listened patiently, usually to inform the inventor that the "solution" he offered to a particular problem had already been tried out by the Engineering Division and found impracticable, or that his "new" device had been tested during the war and discarded. Promoters who had unsuccessfully attempted to foist some unsound idea on private industry, or who had failed to put over a stock company on the strength of some pseudo-inventor's claims, got the ear of a Congressman, and Bane became the "goat." He withstood threats, abuse, and scorn unperturbed, while McCook Field hummed with activity. He was "investigated" by committees of Congress, but always emerged unblemished.

It is difficult for one who has not visited the Field to visualize the diversity of the activities carried on there. The entire equipment problem of the Army Air Corps was under constant study. This comprised everything involved in the makeup of an airplane, including the airplane structure and the air flow about such structure, the engine, the various ignition systems, the battery and magneto, the armament, including fixed machine guns, mechanical and electrical synchronizers (timing devices to allow the bullets to pass between the whirling propeller blades), flexible machine guns, ammunition belt containers and gun sights to allow windage corrections, flexible gun mounts, bomb dropping devices with selective bomb dropping mechanisms, simple and complicated mechanical and electrical bomb sights and wind drift-determination indicators. Also under study was a variety of instruments, including aids to navigation such as turn-and-bank indicators, artificial horizons, gyroscopic compasses, earth inductor compasses such as those used on most successful transoceanic flights, and mapping cameras.

In addition to these projects, the division was responsible for basic research on design of various types of air-craft for various military purposes and for corresponding engines to be used in these aircraft. When it is considered that the light alloy metal used to make the cast alloy head of the Wright Whirlwind motor, together with the method of casting it and the design of the head, were developed at McCook Field after nine unsuccessful efforts, one may understand the character of the research development required of the personnel.

Another survey was conducted, over a period of eight weeks, of finance, research laboratories, office management, and so forth. When the reports had been studied, a Commanding Officers' School was established to make capable organizers and executives of the ranking personnel. The school was patterned along the lines found most successful in private industry.

It was further decided that the innumerable projects of research were too diversified. Although pressure constantly was being brought to bear on Bane to cut out all research, he finally adopted a middle-of-the-road policy which turned much of the work over to private industry and left the personnel at McCook free to concentrate on planes, engines, and military aviation.

A definite program of research procedure soon evolved. First came design and the mock-up model. Then flight models were built, one for sand test to destruction, and one for flight performance. The next step was the building of a few planes for service tests at the different air stations of the United States. Under the hot suns of Texas, or in the winter cold of Michigan at Selfridge Field, the airplanes were given grueling trials.

"Whip the 'bugs' in experimental design under actual service conditions, then go into mass production"—this was the essence of Bane's development policy. That three United States Army planes were able to circumnavigate the earth under climates ranging from polar to tropical— another aviation "first"—was in no small degree due to the researches at McCook under Bane's leadership.

There followed a period of record-smashing. Altitude, endurance, speed records, one after another fell before Army planes attuned for super-performance as the result of painstaking researches at McCook. And while to the stout-hearted Army fliers is due the credit for their stamina and courage, to Bane and his associates must go the credit for making these achievements possible.

Under Bane's guidance, Major Hoffman and his associates developed the parachute that has become standard equipment in the air services of armies and navies throughout the world. Another officer who would be the first to acknowledge Bane as a constant inspiration and source of encouragement to him in his work is Captain A. W. Stevens, whose pioneering aerial photography record is recognized the world over as second to none. And from the research conducted at McCook grew such developments as the Fairchild Aerial Camera Company and Fairchild Aerial Photo Company, both based upon Captain Stevens's work; the air-cooled engine, originally Lawrance's Wright Whirlwind, which was being developed at Dayton when

Lindbergh was making his first solo flight in Texas, then the Pratt & Whitney Wasp, a later development. Major Hoffman's parachute experiments led to the Irving Air Chute Company, and the instrument section at McCook developed the first so-called "cloud flying board," with which McCook pilots, as early as 1922, were making blind flights above the clouds between Dayton and Washington. This research in turn led to the earth-inductor compass used by Lindbergh, Byrd, and many others.

These, then, were only a few of the most outstanding developments to come from the McCook Field group. Bane's pet hobby of "leave your rank outside" and his genius for handling men had built an *esprit de corps* that held together in one smooth-working unit the greatest group of aeronautical experts hitherto assembled.

Before the war, aviation had been in an apathetic state. There had been no market for commercial industry in the air. But now aviation was booming and, in its great need for able engineers and technicians, private industry went to the source of most of aviation's modern advances—McCook Field. One by one the staff was picked off until only a handful was left. At the beginning of World War II there was hardly an important post in the engineering departments of the major aviation companies which was not held by a McCook Field "graduate."

In 1922 Bane resigned from the Army, and his fellow officers gave him a regretful farewell that amply proved their affection and esteem. In his Army career Bane had been criticized for not being "diplomatic" because he would not play Army politics with aeronautical science. To all who knew him, however, the implied derogation was the finest kind of praise. Bane could not be bothered with petty politics. His one concern was fair play and the chance to do his job well.

In private industry Bane became Chief of Technical Staff of the American Aviation Corporation, but he soon longed for the sod of flying fields and the roar of high-speed aviation engines. The smell of gas and oil was perfume to this flying man. But in the years that followed, while aviation was in the pre-Lindbergh doldrums, Bane never lost faith in its future. "Stick to it, men," he advised his former co-workers during a visit to McCook Field in 1926. "You are in the finest training school in the country. Aviation is coming, and you will be the masters of its destiny."

He was out of the Army and had become an industrial executive behind a desk in Manhattan, but in his heart Bane took McCook Field to New York with him. The work he did for American Aviation Corporation was undoubtedly important. He advised on all equipment, aircraft purchases, airline operations, etc., and it was on his recommendation that American Aviation bought the airline from Miami to Havana and South America—a line that was to be the first link in the vast air chain of Pan American Airways. After a life of hard work this was Bane's chance to relax a bit from the stern demands of the Army at McCook, to work at a not too arduous job at good financial return—but he was, frankly, not happy in an office.

Bane, whose ability to handle men had welded his personnel of temperamental aviation stars and engineering experts into a close-knit, productive group, found it difficult to get along with bankers and men of finance.

"What do bankers know about aviation?" he would complain, sadly. "They don't understand it." He was restive, uncomfortable. He was potentially an important factor in the postwar aviation boom, but at a desk away from fliers and planes he fretted and lost interest. And he felt a great moral obligation to the public, though his job was that of technical adviser only. He worried whether the public was being dealt with fairly, whether his position was justified, whether aviation was in good hands . . . taking, in his own characteristic way, the burdens of a growing industry as his personal responsibility. All this may perhaps have hastened Bane's death from a brain tumor while still a comparatively young man.

One dream was never realized: his belief that aviation needed a great central research laboratory where there might be concentrated the men and means for dealing with the fundamental research problems of the industry; a combined Rockefeller Institute and General Motors research laboratory of aeronautics. Never a politician or wire-puller, Thurman Bane did not realize his dream. One with less executive and technical genius but a talent for diplomatic maneuvering might have wangled it. Bane felt that the obvious, the right, and the necessary needed no stressing. And so he dreamed—for once, the man of action became purely the visionary—of a vast research organization, backed by men of vision and nourished by adequate appro-

priations. He pictured a group supplied by the entire industry with all the modern apparatus of science. He saw a
unified staff of the quiet, thinking men whose work and
brains built the science of aeronautics. Perhaps, too, he
dreamed of the old days at McCook, when he guided the
work at the crucible of aviation technology, engine roar
in his ears and the propeller slip stream whipping at his
face . . . a dream that lingered as he sighed for the days
when production, dividends, and balance sheets had no
place in the picture.

But his thoughts were not all idle daydreams of the past
or the future. Bane stated correctly the status of aviation
in 1930, the year of his death. He explained the lack of a
co-ordinated research bureau this way: during the War
there was no time to organize such an outfit, and following
the War there occurred a period of deflation when the
infant aviation industry was too busy keeping afloat to
think of the importance of pure and applied research. Then
the Lindbergh flight and similar achievements threw aviation suddenly into the public spotlight. Mushroom companies sprang up overnight; everyone wanted to own a
share of something—it mattered little what—connected
with the aviation industry. Air stocks boomed and there
arrived the aeronautical commercial and banking age, in
the first blush of which expansion was too rapid to be sound
and was out of all proportion to the state of technical and
scientific progress.

Before he died Bane felt that aviation was getting its
second wind. It was reappraising its situation and settling

down to business. Research and development would follow naturally upon the growth of a sound, productive industry, as they had in the automotive industry.

And Bane's picture of the future, which he never lived to see realized, is another tribute to his vision. He did not agree with those who held that the lighter-than-air craft were the solution to future transatlantic flying. The investment in the dirigible and the operating costs of the pay load were, he thought, disproportionate. His picture of the aircraft of the future might have been drawn from present-day accomplishments that are already being surperseded: he forecast a flying boat, capable of carrying fifty or more persons and designed for speedy ocean travel. He ventured this prophecy years before Pan American and Imperial Airways successfully spanned the Atlantic and Pacific with commercial transport flying boats. And his visionary planes of the future checked, almost in every detail, with our present-day airliners. Today they roar over vast continents and ocean wastes, memorials not only to those men who were directly responsible for their existence but also to Thurman H. Bane whose planning and vision helped make such aircraft possible.

Chapter 3

VIKING OF THE AIR

Erik Nelson

One of the greatest epic adventures in the history of man's conquest of the air was the Round-the-World Flight of the Army Air Service. On September 28, 1924, the twelve-cylinder Liberties of the Douglas Cruisers came roaring to a landing that marked the successful conclusion of the first circumnavigation of the globe by air.

In these days of huge, fast transports, of aircraft equipped with several powerful engines, of daily transoceanic flights, of organized meteorological data, of radio direction finders, radar, and loran, it is easy to forget the greatness of that earlier, earth-circling achievement in the pageant of aviation progress. The flight was made in ships which, even though they represented the very best of their time, we would consider woefully inadequate. Two of the four Army planes which started out completed the trip of some 26,345 miles. Open cockpit biplanes with few of

45

the present-day instruments, powered by water-cooled, war-built Liberty engines, they were subjected to every hazard of every country, from the ice-capped mountains of the Aleutian Islands to the blistering deserts of India, Baluchistan, Persia, and Iraq.

The history of that flight has been written in the head-lines of the world's newspapers. But certain facts are not so widely known. Among the group of Army officers who first conceived and enthusiastically backed the idea was Lieutenant Erik Nelson. On the original World Flight Committee in Washington was again the name of Erik Nelson. When, after long consideration, Donald W. Douglas was selected as the builder of the Round-the-World Cruisers, it was Lieutenant Nelson who was author-ized to supervise the construction of the first experimental world cruisers. For Nelson was then known as one of the finest pilots and most able practical engineers in the Army Air Service. Thus, it was Nelson who watched every strut and wire being put into place on the new Cruisers, Nelson who first test-hopped one of the ships as a land plane and later tested it when pontoons were put into place.

On the flight itself, Erik Nelson was responsible for engine maintenance as Engineer Officer, perhaps the most vital single job of any crew member. The following story of Nelson's selection furnishes an interesting sidelight upon his reputation. When the final preparations for the flight were being made by the Air Service Planning Division, discussion over selection of flight-crew members was in-tense. Individual knowledge, confidence, responsibility, and all-round resourcefulness were carefully considered, and the relative abilities of each candidate as flier and navigator were weighed. When four of the officers in the Chief of Air Service's office each put a slip of paper in a sealed envelope, naming the man he thought most likely to come through on the flight, each paper bore the name of Erik Nelson.

And Nelson came through, proving to be the mainstay of that great adventure, even though the betting among Air Service officers was so high that not more than one plane would make the round trip.

It was in 1921 that a tall, sandy-haired man, already partly bald, stood in the doorway of the Flying Section Office at McCook Field. He had the figure of a West Pointer, and a friendly grin lit his ruddy face as he stood diffidently fingering his helmet and goggles.

"I'm Nelson," he said, "Erik Nelson. The C. O. has assigned me as Officer in Charge of Planes and Maintenance. Where do I start in the Flying Section?" He spoke with a decided Swedish accent, which had persisted in spite of twelve years spent in America. This was his self-introduction. He was presented to the "greasenecks" in the hangars as "Swede" Nelson, "the best engineer officer in the Army Air Service. You can't put anything over on this bird!"

It wasn't hard to believe. "Swede" Nelson looked the part of a man who was infinitely more at home gazing into the innards of an airplane engine than into office records. His brown, capable hands were obviously more fitted to a wrench than a pencil. And that was hardly surprising, for

Nelson's experience as sailor before the mast, mechanic, garageman, and aviation mechanic long preceded his career in the cockpit of a plane. Those same practical experiences, which helped make him the valuable practical engineer that he was, made him at home with the boys in the hangar and a bit shy and retiring with his brother officers.

Both the "homing" instinct for which Nelson was noted and his engineering genius came to him as his birthright, so to speak. The son of Erik Nelson, a Swedish engineer, he was born in Stockholm in June 1888. There he attended public and high schools, as well as night courses in a technical school where he learned the rudiments of mechanics. It was from his father, however, that he received most of his first knowledge of engineering. Together father and son would go for long walks, during which Nelson, senior, passed to his son much of the engineering lore that was to be the foundation upon which Erik's later practical experience was built.

"It isn't what you do—it's how you do it," his father used to say, and Erik has held the same motto ever since.

In 1905 Erik spent a summer on a training ship, and when he was seventeen he shipped as a sailor before the mast. On a Swedish barque he saw England, then crossed the Atlantic to Guadeloupe. He voyaged up and down the coast of South America, and visited the United States for the first time. And though he knew Swedish, German, and French, he was convinced, from his first cruise, that English would be essential and so he applied himself, without textbooks, using only magazines for his guides, to learn the language.

After his return home he shipped on various English boats and made two trips around the world, long before he dreamed of duplicating the journey in a fraction of the time by air. After some four years' sailing before the mast, Erik was paid off in Hamburg, Germany, in 1909.

Word had spread that sailors were well paid for working on racing yachts in America, so Nelson, now twenty, shipped for America. He landed in Hoboken with thirty-five dollars, a paper suitcase, and a canvas bag his entire personal possessions. He found work as a rigger in a Greenwich shipyard, then found the place he was after on a racing yacht. When fall came he was again looking for work. A job offered itself as rubber and swimming instructor in a well-known New York Turkish bath, and Erik took it, losing twelve pounds in ten days from the constant heat. He resigned and found a brief theatrical engagement, his splendid physique making him an ideal Roman centurion in Hammerstein's production of *Salome*. Erik's job was to stand guard, wearing sword, shield, and helmet, in the banquet hall while Salome did her dance of the seven veils.

That began and ended Nelson's stage career. His next position was with A. T. Demarest & Company, one of the leading automobile companies of the day. He remained with this firm until 1911, there gaining some of his first experience with engines.

A summer was spent at the Indian Harbor Yacht Club in Greenwich, where Erik was in charge of launches and the garage. Various jobs followed, including occasional work for the Lancia automobile company. Unknowingly, Erik was gradually preparing himself for his real work—in aviation. In Mineola Nelson tested cars at the old speedway, and it was here that he first became interested in aviation, watching the planes there.

"But my first bona-fide job in aviation," Nelson says, "was down in Miami where I worked as a 'greaseneck' for Victor Vernon on a Curtiss 'F' Boat during the winter of '13 and '14. Though I had left a fairly good garage business for this job, the season was poor, and I was left flat on the beach."

Without their last month's salaries Erik and a buddy bummed their way back to New York by train and steamer, arriving with twenty-two cents between them.

From that time on, his mind was on aviation. He took whatever jobs offered, working for the Lancia Company, then for the Curtiss Aeroplane Company, all the while his mind fixed on the future day when he, too, would fly. So he continued to work with planes and automobiles until America entered the war.

In February 1917, Erik was working for the Curtiss Company in Buffalo. There he made his first attempt to enlist in the Aviation Section, Signal Officers' Reserve Corps, and was turned down. In July he quit the Curtiss Company and was offered a job taking care of the blimps being built by the Goodyear Company in Akron, but decided to stay with the heavier-than-air crowd. He next went to work as a mechanic with the American Trans-Oceanic Company at Port Washington, L. I. This was an outfit financed by the late Rodman Wanamaker and a group of sportsmen who wanted to make a transatlantic flight. Although the plane they had built never made the attempt because of the war, and the venture came to nothing, it was an odd coincidence that Nelson should have been connected with such a venture, in view of his later career as a pioneer in transoceanic flying.

A second time Erik tried to enlist in the Signal Officers' Reserve Corps but was turned down. He went to Canada and tried to enter the Royal Air Force, but his twenty-nine years were against him and he was refused, both in Toronto and New York. His third and last attempt to crash the Signal Officers' Reserve Corps proved successful, and he enlisted on October 15, 1917, at Hazlehurst Field, where he had so often watched planes flying years before.

Once in the Army, Nelson's progress from hangar mechanic to one of the best cross-country pilots in the Air Service was rapid. In January 1918, he graduated from the Cornell University Ground School and was assigned to Ellington Field, Texas. He finished primary training there and went on to the Advanced Bombing School at the same field, moved on to assistant in charge of the Advanced Cross Country Stage, and finally to the Acrobatic Stage, of which he took charge a few months later. When the Armistice came Erik was shifted from instruction to testing and engineering, the rest of his Army career being spent in this work.

In January and February 1919, Nelson acted as pilot and engineering officer on a four-thousand-mile trip known as the Gulf-to-Pacific Flight and return. During this trip the fliers photographed the Grand Canyon and were, he believes, the first aviators to fly down into the Canyon. In July 1919, Erik piloted one of the four planes sent on a recruiting trip throughout the country. They stopped at seventy-two cities, without a single forced landing—another tribute to Nelson's ability as an engineering officer who could be depended upon to bring his squadron back every time with the absolute minimum of plane and engine trouble.

The following year Nelson was transferred to Kelly Field and made Engineering Officer of the Twentieth Aero Squadron, and in May he went to Mitchel Field to supervise and participate in the Army's first cross-country flight to Alaska—the New York to Nome flight.

Lieutenant St. Clair Street, one of America's foremost aviators and the officer responsible for much of the unsung work in the arranging of the World Flight, was the commander. Erik Nelson had the responsibility of maintaining the craft and engines as Engineering Officer, and acted as co-pilot with Lieutenant C. C. Nutt in one of the planes; DH's which had been returned from overseas.

This project was, at the time, an extremely difficult feat to accomplish because of the problems involved. Today, almost thirty years later, the importance of the Alaskan flight can be more easily appreciated, as well as the difficulties the pioneer airmen faced. It was invaluable as a tactical test of cold-weather flying, demonstrating what fliers might expect from oils in sub-zero weather, ice on wings, etc. The planes carried photographic equipment and did valuable work in charting the territory, hitherto virgin to air travel. The importance of this work in the light of subsequent developments, both military and commercial, has been demonstrated. In time of war Alaska becomes a jumping-off place for a possible emergency, while in time of peace Alaska's internal transportation system relies on aviation as a vital link. In a country almost inaccessible for a large part of the year the airplane furnishes the only rapid means of transportation in many cases, its only alternative being the slow and toilsome trek by dogsled. Since that time, Sir Hubert Wilkins has used Point Barrow as a base for his polar explorations, the Russian fliers stopped at Alaska in their polar flights, and an elaborate network of defense bases was organized and constructed during World War II. For these and other ventures it was essential to know the conditions and topography. Once again the Army had pointed the way.

With the full responsibility for the successful performance of planes and engines on his broad shoulders during this trip, Erik Nelson kept his wartime planes in the air without any forced landings due to engine trouble, and after 11,000 miles of flying brought them home intact. In addition to his engineering genius, Nelson possessed an almost uncanny "homing instinct" that was the despair and envy of his flying mates. The nose of his plane seemed always to be dead on the objective, and his line of flight, when charted on airways maps, was almost invariably the straight-line course. In those days before two-way radios, direction finders, beams, and blind flying instruments, Nelson, Viking of the air, could be depended upon to lead the boys home.

And Nelson, with luck and skill, could "take it." On the return from Nome, Lieutenant Street landed his plane on a soft field in Hazleton, British Columbia. Erik, who had been riding in the rear cockpit, slid down the fuselage to the tail of the plane, in an attempt to keep it from nosing over on its back. One of the wheels stuck in the soft ground, however, and the plane went up on its nose, catapulting Nelson through the air for about twenty-five feet. All onlookers expected to pick him up in a stretcher, badly hurt. But Erik got up on his own two sturdy legs, uninjured, and was able to repair the smashed landing gear without delaying the next flight.

When the Army Air Service planned a flight to Puerto Rico, it was Erik Nelson again who was appointed Engineering Officer, ordered to Kelly Field to get six DH's ready for the flight, and teamed up with Lieutenant Delmar Dunton as co-pilot. The six planes made their flight and returned to Washington at the beginning of April 1923 without mishap.

When plans for the Army's World Flight were begun, Erik Nelson was not only a logical contender on the basis of his record and experience, but he had already done some preparatory work in planning the flight with Lieutenant C. C. Crumrin, who was also assigned to the project. And though Nelson had been one of the first to advocate sending American aviators around the world, and had been on

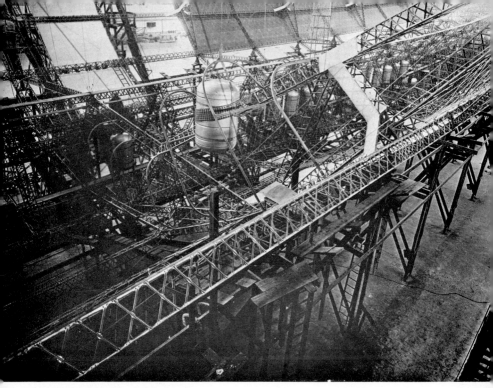

Interior of the *Shenandoah*

NC-4 in flight

Sperry messenger plane (early 1920's), with three-cylinder Lawrance engine

Col. Bane with the de Bothezat helicopter (left to right: Dr. Eremeff, Bane, and Dr. de Bothezat)

Round-the-World flight arriving New York, Sept. 8, 1924

Round-the-World fliers: (left to right) Capt. L. H. Smith, Lts. Ogden, Nelson, Wade, Harding, and Arnold

Igor Sikorsky pointing to the engine nacelle of an early biplane. Prof. Klemin stands third from right

Capt. Stevens (right) with his pilot, Lt. Corkille

World's-record long-distance picture, taken from 23,000 feet

St. Helena Range

MT. SHASTA
331.2 Miles from camera
Lat. 41°24'28"
Long. 122°11'45"

Suisun Bay   Mt. Diablo   Sacramento River   Sacramento Valley

Francisco Bay

San Jose

Santa Clara Valley

San Martin

Santa Cruz Mountains   Gilroy

Southern Pacific

Southern Pacific R. R.

Pajaro River   Joda Lake   Pajaro River

California Central R. R.

San Juan Bautista

Position of Airplane–23000 ft.
Lat. 36°36'17"   (8 Miles east
Long 121°56'27" of Salinas.)

Mission San Juan Bautista

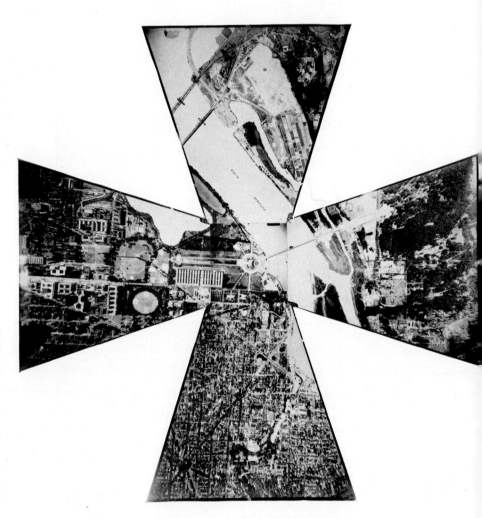

Five-lens work of an aerial camera (transformed prints assembled)

Lt. Don Bruner, pioneering "night bird"

Early wingtip landing-light and flare

"Dummy Joe" — hero of a thousand jumps before "a man alive"

Jump with the triangular vented chute

Free-fall jump

Sand-testing a Vought VE-8 (reverse loading technique)

Stout "Sky Car" (note forward wheel to prevent nosing-over)

Kalec, Inc.

Bill Stout and his "Sky Car"

First Ford-Stout trimotor plane

McDonnell's first flight from a battleship without a catapult, 1918-1919

Orville Wright and Charles Lawrance

The Model L-2 Motor

LAWRANCE MODEL L-2 MOTOR
Front View

Wright Aeronautical Corp.

Prototype of the Wright Whirlwind engine

the first committee to study and make plans for the flight, he never expected actually to take part in the flight itself. Even after he had tested the first Douglas Cruiser built under his supervision to Army specifications, Nelson was quite sure that he would not be among the pilots on the epic adventure, for he had already taken part in more than his share of great flights, and the policy of the Air Service was to divide such honors as equally as possible among the best flying personnel. There were scores of pilots who met the requirements of character, courage, and initiative—all eager to be among the immortal four crews—but when final decisions were made Erik Nelson's name was on every list.

On epic flights such as this one the success of the venture —and the life of the flier—depends not so much on the big things, which are obviously watched over, but upon the comparatively insignificant details. A bit of carelessness, an engine failure, a crash, these are apt to be responsible for the greatest percentage of mishaps or tragedies of the air. Seldom does a plane's wing rip off, plunging the plane to earth. This was true even in those early days in aeronautics. But a broken oil line, a blown gasket, a mechanic's failure to replace an oil cap or tighten a nut—these are the minor details that make major failures. And the only safeguard against them is someone who sees and knows, a man with the super-ability and eternal vigilance of Erik Nelson. "Never let your plane down," Erik would say, "and it'll never let you down." And that was his invariable policy.

No matter how hurried, how harassed or tired he might be, his first thought was always for his ship and for those under his responsibility.

The leading airplane engine of the time was the Liberty, and it was selected as the motive power for the world-girdling planes. Its reliability had been demonstrated on many long, grinding, cross-country flights in all kinds of weather. Also, it was the leading American-made engine. The airplane to make the flight did not yet exist, the planners felt. So after going over the entire list of airplane manufacturers who could meet the rigid specifications of government-supervised construction, they asked Donald W. Douglas of Santa Monica, designer of the famous Martin bomber, to design and build the Round-the-World Cruisers.

Douglas supplied the theoretical knowledge and Nelson, as government supervisor, the practical. The two men fought long, hard, and often while the first experimental model was being built, but out of their discussions arose a great respect and warm friendship that still exists.

The engine was, of course, Erik's first concern. In the *Engineering Report of the Round-the-World Flight* Nelson wrote:

> "The engine situation is always the most serious one in any undertaking of this nature. Regardless of how good the planes are, or how well everything is planned and organized, or the ability of the pilots, when the engine stops, in most cases, the flight ends right there. It is seldom that a forced landing can be made in a strange country or over great bodies of water without

damage to the plane. Not only the lives of the personnel are at stake, but also the honor of the Service and the whole Nation, and no effort should be spared in preparing the engines to insure success of the project. Usually it is a small thing that lets you down, and not a big one."

By way of illustration Nelson clinched his argument with this specific instance:

"Lack of care in assembly of one engine almost caused a forced landing to Plane No. 2 on the flight between Greenland and Labrador. The gasket between the oil pump and crankcase blew out where the oil lead passes through, due to the fact that the nuts holding the pumps to the crankcase were not tightened up. Less than two gallons of oil were left out of twenty at the end of this flight which lasted six hours and fifty-five minutes. Had the flight encountered head winds on this run, the plane would never have reached its destination."

Another example was the failure of the engine in Plane No. 4 just before coming into Karachi, India, which occurred after 115 hours of very hard flying. The precise cause of the failure was not known. Either a valve had dropped down into a cylinder or the valve stem broke just below the head. The head of the valve was found in the engine cowling, having been knocked through the crankcase. Lack of time made it impossible for a complete inspection of the engine on that leg of the flight.

Nelson's engineering report is an illuminating record of advanced planning for every possible emergency. And Nelson's actions throughout the flight explain, too, his eternal vigilance, as when the fliers hopped from their triumphant welcome in Paris to Croydon Field, England. Nelson, clad in British Army shorts and an O. D. shirt, hopped out of his plane and, while Royal Air Force mechanicians began going over it, Erik, too, was strumming a flying wire here, testing a strut with a resounding slap and thud with his palm, crawling under the fuselage to inspect the landing gear and tail surfaces. He was concerned only for his plane, while a surging crowd of English aviation fans eagerly waited outside the police lines to shake his hand, touch his helmet, or press their autograph books upon him.

Though not ungrateful for the reception, Nelson was totally unimpressed; his first and last thoughts were for his plane. Not too tired to glow with pride, he insisted on taking his welcomers, among whom was the author, on a personally conducted tour of inspection over every point of the plane. He summed up the inspection by saying: "Not bad condition for a ship that's flown three quarters of the way around the world, eh?" Which was, in itself, an understatement, for his ship's fabric was tight as a drum, its surfaces shining as though it had been just rolled out of the hangar for a flight. There was no sign of those 15,000 grueling miles. His winged steed got as much attention as though it were flesh and blood.

Lieutenants Smith, Wade, Arnold, Harding, and Ogden, his companions on the flight, said that no matter how many banquets or welcoming celebrations Nelson attended, no matter how late he might have been out on the previous night, he was always one of the first men around the planes in the morning. Clad in overalls he would be tuning up his engine, tightening a wire or strut, testing his controls— leaving nothing to chance. It was small wonder that his plane never let him down.

But the strain of the long grind eventually began to tell on the hardy Norseman. When he was riding in to London in a Royal Air Force car, through streets crowded with Britons out to do homage to the intrepid American heroes of the air, Nelson fell asleep as he mumbled a request that a stop be made at a haberdasher's to get him a white shirt. He had with him for the dinner to be given that evening in honor of the American fliers by the British Royal Air Force only the O. D. shirt he was wearing.

Most of the record has been recounted elsewhere of the Round-the-World Flight and the triumphant return to the United States via the perilous crossing of the North Atlantic from Brough, England, by way of Iceland and Greenland. The fliers' arrival in New York and their tumultuous welcome in Seattle, the starting point, has also been told. That there were not a million persons swarming Mitchel Field, New York, when the fliers landed, instead of thousands, that there was not the wildly abandoned, typical New York welcome of ticker tape, shredded paper, and parade can only be ascribed to the fact that the public was not then psychologically geared to appreciate the scope of the exploit. The term "air-minded" had not yet been coined. Too, the flight was an achievement of an organization—the Army—rather than of an individual, and it is difficult to glorify an organization. It was, perhaps, an indirect compliment and a tribute in itself that the public expected great things from our Army to the point of almost taking them for granted.

The World Flight, also, was the last outstanding feat of the old, water-cooled, Liberty engine. Well as it had performed, the famous war baby and last of the line of American aircraft engines that had served the Allied Air Fleet was soon to yield to lighter, more powerful engines of advanced design. Already were sounding the first birth cries of the air-cooled engine which was just then coming out of the laboratory under the guidance of Charles Lawrance, ready to fly into the spotlight with Lindbergh, Chamberlin, Byrd, and other transatlantic fliers.

After the Round-the-World Flight, Nelson was assigned to the Douglas plant as government inspector. Two years later he reluctantly left the Air Service to plunge into commercial aviation. It was a step that worked out well for Erik. With the Boeing Company he became an important figure in the rapid development of commercial aviation. His judgment of air transport companies, based upon his technical judgment of planes and men, was good. For several years he moved with Boeing through mergers and consolidations which carried the Boeing Company to the fore in aircraft manufacture and, for a while, airlines operation.

Yet, sailing ships had not passed forever out of Nelson's life. Several years before World War II began Inglis M. Uppercu, New York agent for Cadillac Motors, invited Nelson and a group of friends down to a Hudson River shipyard where new Diesel engines were being installed in an old, square-rigged, Swedish sailing ship he had bought. Showing them over the ship, he pointed with some pride to the comfortable owner's quarters furnished in luxurious style. Nelson rambled off by himself in the direction of the forecastle. Here the party found him browsing about, intently examining the crew's quarters and making inquiry about the remodeled sailing gear. When they asked him about his interest in that part of the ship, the "Swede" smiled.

"You see," he said, "twenty-five years ago I sailed as a cadet sailor before the mast on this good ship. So I was just browsing around"—his smile broadened—"I thought some of the boys might still be aboard."

Chapter 4

NIGHT BIRDS

Donald L. Bruner

"The local powerhouse has failed. Telephone, beacons, radios, floodlights, and boundary lights are out of commission. There's a black stretch of landing area in front of the administration building darker than the night. Airport officials are running helter-skelter with candles and kerosene lamps. Overhead in the dark two motors are throttled to moaning cadence while puzzled airmen on the big airliner try to figure out the blackness and silence below. . . . Then the big decision to land is made in the cockpit up forward.

"Someone comes to life below. A flare and a can of gas are lighted at each end of the long runway. The long fingers of the plane's landing lights probe the darkness, seeking bottom. The ship swings lower and lower. Then a long easy glide, with motors half throttled, to be cut when the wheels touch the ground.

"Tension is in the air. With only a dim estimate of the

length of clear runway ahead a sigh is heaved when the ship stops rolling. . . ." (From a news story by Major Al Williams, New York *World-Telegram*, September 23, 1937.)

There, in a news story of a tricky landing without lights at the airport, might have been the story of a great air tragedy but for a slightly built, dark young man named Donald L. Bruner. Might have been . . . except for the fact that without a Donald Bruner there might have been no commercial air transport at all, certainly no night flights at all.

In our present stage of aeronautical development with transport planes roaring aloft on regular, scheduled flights day and night, it may perhaps not be easy to visualize a time when all planes were automatically grounded at dusk. And yet that time was comparatively recent. It was in the years immediately following the First World War, when other McCook Field "graduates" were making their various important contributions to man's mastery of the air. At that time there was only one who foresaw the necessity of making the airplane independent of light or darkness, only one who possessed both the courage and the driving conviction that kept him plugging away for four long years of arduous and dangerous trial-and-error experiments at risk of life and limb so that planes might have "eyes" at night. Not only was Captain Bruner the only one who pioneered in this vital field, he was the only one who felt the urgent necessity for such pioneering. As a result, today every night hop to Chicago or Los Angeles, every night air-mail flight, every night Air Force maneuver is a tribute to his work, a monument to his perseverance.

Don Bruner had a fixation on the problem of night flying and with good reason. The story goes back to a tragic night on a lonely Texas flying field, when young Bruner stood bitterly contemplating the charred and splintered wreckage of a plane, the result of accidental ignition of a wingtip landing flare on a forced landing. Burned and mangled within the grisly debris was the body of Bruner's best friend, a sacrifice to inadequate equipment.

There in the darkness, with the pungent odor of the smoking wreck still in his nostrils, the young flier resolved that, if his efforts could prevent it, no further accidents like this should occur. He would make night flying not only possible but practical and safe. Bruner was not the flamboyant or demonstrative type. He said nothing of his decision, but deep within the slim, dark, studious young Lieutenant was born an unalterable determination that was all the stronger for his quiet reserve.

Colonel Thurman H. Bane had no way of knowing this when, about a year afterward, in 1919, he was making a tour of inspection at McCook Field. The routine business of the aircraft research center was in progress. The sky was vibrant with the drone of planes swirling and dipping overhead. Near the hangars mechanics were tuning up other ships. Motors were roaring as they prepared for the take-off. Still other planes were landing at the far end of the field and taxiing toward the hangars.

As Bane's keen eyes wandered over the field they were drawn to one plane approaching the ground. He watched it as it settled to the field in a perfect three-point landing, then turned and taxied to the hangars, where the test pilot unsnapped his safety belt and clambered down from the cockpit of the plane.

Following his usual habit of giving praise where praise was due, Colonel Bane strolled over to the ship. The pilot was Second Lieutenant Don Bruner, who had just joined the McCook Field group, and who had done nothing, up to that time, to distinguish himself other than the satisfactory performance of the routine tasks assigned him.

"That was a nice landing you made," the C. O. remarked.

"Thank you, sir," Bruner said. "But, of course, it's daylight now."

Bane was slightly puzzled. "What has daylight got to do with it?"

"Well—" Bruner said, "it's easy enough to make a good landing in daylight, Colonel Bane. But getting down all right in the dark is pretty hard." Bruner thought he saw his opportunity and was off on his pet subject. "You know, sir, I did a lot of night flying in Texas and now, when I'm landing in daylight, I try to imagine how it would be making the same landing at night. I figure we'll soon have to fly and land at night so I'm trying to find out all I can about it now."

"Trying to break your neck, are you?" Bane said tersely, and prepared to swing on his heel to continue his inspection trip. But there was something glowing in the young Lieutenant's eyes that held him.

"Colonel Bane—please—may I have official permission to make some experiments in night flying? I know something about it and I have some ideas I'd like to try out. I'm sure I can work out a system . . ." and Bruner was off on an eager explanation. After a few minutes Bane cut him short. "Forget it," he said, and left to complete his inspection tour.

This was Bruner's first attempt to get official permission for his night-flying experiments. "Forget it" was the one thing that Bruner was unable to do, any more than he could forget the ghastly sight of his friend's blackened, crumpled plane on that field in Texas. But he said nothing of this to his commanding officer. He merely waited for his next opportunity, just as Major Hoffman, to whose section Bruner was assigned, had doggedly pursued the fulfillment of his dream of the parachute.

The young Air Corps Lieutenant had received night-flying lessons as part of his Army training. However, this had been at camps where war conditions were simulated, war being the only reason for which flights after dark were even considered. At Ellington Field, Texas, where he had done some night work under Major Rudolph ("Shorty") Schroeder, then Captain Schroeder, Bruner's training had been merely the routine of familiarizing pilots with the scanty equipment—such as wing flares—then available, rather than the development of completely new lighting materials. But war, in 1918–19, just after the close of the First World War, seemed a very remote possibility.

So, with no war in view and commercial aviation almost nonexistent, it is not remarkable that Army officers were uniformly convinced that the place for a plane, after dark, was in its hangar. And until Don Bruner set to work that was where, except in a few negligible instances, the planes remained.

When Bruner applied for an assignment to the equipment section of the Electrical Branch at McCook he was twenty-six years old. Four years earlier he had received his B. S. E. E. from Iowa State University, achieving his engineering degree with the aid of a scholarship. Then he obtained some practical and design experience in electrical work with General Electric Company. Practical aeronautics he learned at Army training camps, and a course in aeronautical engineering was taken by him at M. I. T. Such an educational background was valuable. Bruner's superiors were not in favor of risking such a man in the dangerous and apparently foolhardy pursuit of night-flying knowledge.

In the short time Bruner had been at the field he had acquired a reputation as a safe pilot, one who was cautious, deliberate, and observant, obeying all the rules and never attempting the spectacular. He made friends, in spite of the fact that he was a somewhat morose person and verged on the scholarly type rather than the social mixer. Yet for all his reserve his associates liked him. Long after the others had closed their desks and left their tasks for the day Don Bruner would remain, poring over books and charts. In conversation with a group he would lead the talk inevitably into wholly technical matters. He was a man with a mission, entirely absorbed in his work and possessing few or no outside interests.

Lieutenant Bruner's first failure to win permission for

his experiments from Colonel Bane did not shake his resolve. He knew that permission must come from Bane and Major Hoffman, and he had no illusions that it would be easy to secure that sanction. But time after time his efforts to convert his superiors to the realization of the importance of night flying met with scant attention. Still he maintained his dogged persistence—a surprisingly tenacious persistence in view of the fact that he was, in all other respects, far from the rugged, aggressive, driving type of fighter. And his unflinching determination finally won him one concession: Colonel Bane agreed to listen seriously to his arguments. It may have been only a gesture to satisfy Bruner's constant hammering, perhaps simply to keep him quiet, but Bane gave the young Lieutenant his attention while Bruner poured out his conviction that night flying must be an inevitable development for future commercial flying, and that by serving the commercial industry-to-come the Army would benefit as well, in the long run.

Bane heard him out, then summarized his views. "Flying in daylight," he said, "is hazardous enough. But that's our job—and we must take the chances that go with it. Our problem now is to work toward the perfection of regular daylight flying. With the vast field for improvement and development there, we can't afford to bother with night flying which might be remotely useful.

"You've been carefully trained and educated, Lieutenant. I'm concerned for your personal safety, both for your own sake and for your value to the government. I can't allow you to take great and unnecessary risks. And what of those on the ground? How about their necks? No, Lieutenant, I admire your ambition and determination, but I'm afraid it's too foolhardy to attempt. Landing in the daytime is difficult enough. My advice to you is to dismiss the whole idea."

Again Bruner was turned down. More aggressive men than he might have been permanently squelched by such a blanket refusal as Bane had given. But Bane was to learn the quality of that determination he had praised. Don Bruner waited only as long as he thought diplomatic, then was back to renew the attack, this time with an argument that has since become a classic one in aviation circles.

"Suppose," he told his chief, "that our railroads and steamships ran only during the day. What sort of schedules could they keep? How much financial support could they enlist? What inventive genius would they attract? In an air service based upon daylight flights alone there is an average loss of twelve hours out of the twenty-four. There can be only a half service offered. But with planes flying night and day their efficiency will be increased one hundred per cent over present standards, and any reasonable schedules can be maintained."

So went his eternal arguments. Hammer, drive, and bore, wear down by sheer repetition, impress by constant reiteration of his points—this was Bruner's campaign as time after time he spoke, his dark, thin face alight with the fire of his one interest. It is a considerable tribute to Bane's tolerance that he listened and refrained from becoming overly irritated at Bruner's maddening persistence on a subject that the commanding officer did not yet believe in. But listen he did, and Bruner never let up.

Eventually Bane grew more interested. Some of Bruner's shots had found their mark. But he still was not convinced that Bruner should risk his neck experimenting. No man, however, can indefinitely withstand a barrage like that leveled on Bane by the young Lieutenant. Grudgingly, Bane consented to some experiments in night flying, but only on the condition that Bruner would not attempt them at Mc-Cook Field. And giving his consent, Bane, to cover his misgivings in allowing Bruner to embark on this dangerous enterprise, finished off with: "Go ahead—break your neck your own way!"

Bruner's exultant ardor was undampened even when he found that his friends at McCook Field were as reluctant as his C. O. to support enthusiastically his night-flying experiments. Pity and ridicule were blended in their attitudes. Why bother to increase the hours and the dangers of a job that was already too dangerous and too arduous? They looked upon him as a "nut," a likable "nut" perhaps, but a tilter at the windmill of darkness, astride a rickety Rosinante, his plane—a Curtiss JN-4 or "Jenny"—so out of date and decrepit that no one wanted to fly it, even in daylight.

Nevertheless, Bruner prepared to take his ancient crate to Wilbur Wright Field, eight miles away, for his experiments. It was an odd coincidence of fate, perhaps, that the quiet studious young man should begin the work that everyone branded as a crazy, foolhardy stunt on the very same spot where two bicycle mechanics named Wright had once gone stolidly about an even crazier, more foolhardy experiment that they had believed in.

Perhaps he felt the strength of the Wrights' convictions on that ground where they, scarcely twenty years before, had endured greater ridicule and greater risks in trying to do that which man had never done before. As night after night he made his experiments, took his risks, with his mind so firmly fixed on his goal, he—like all pioneers before him —became impervious to ridicule, criticism, or minor inconveniences.

Much more than by the witticisms of his friends, he was bothered by the necessity of flying his outmoded plane from McCook to Wilbur Wright Field while it was still daylight and getting it back early the next morning, in order not to violate the Colonel's orders to have the ship back at the field where it belonged and ready for duty the next day.

Bruner wanted to keep his first flight a secret, because he, more than anyone else, appreciated the difficulties and the likelihood of failure. But this was out of the question, for the very ridicule he had received had stimulated enough interest to collect a small crowd to watch Don make his first attempt at landing without ground floodlights.

In so far as possible, Bruner took no unnecessary chances. The night he chose was moonless and overcast, but otherwise conditions for flying were excellent. Around the dimly lit hangar at one end clustered the little crowd, skeptical but curious. From some distance away the outline of the plane, standing near the hangar, could hardly be distinguished. On nearer approach the plane and the details of

Don's first device for night landing became visible. This consisted of an ordinary automobile headlight, fastened none too securely to the ship.

At last the engine was tuned up. Don, smiling, climbed aboard and the crowd withdrew, giving the plane a wide berth.

Bruner's confidence was not reflected in the onlookers. There was tension in the watching group. These experienced and hardened skeptics felt a catch in their throats as this young Lieutenant started riding for what seemed an almost certain crash.

The take-off was good. Although the plane was lost to the sight of the observers long before it got off the ground, they soon heard it circling above their heads. Twice more the sound of the motor swelled and died away overhead. Then someone in the crowd shouted, "There he is. He's landing now!"

At the far end of the field a faint yellow light drifted toward the ground. Breathlessly the crowd waited while the distance between the light and the faint outline of the horizon decreased. Then the light bobbed along on the ground for a short distance and stood motionless. At least Don had not cracked up.

As the crowd streamed across the field and approached the plane they found Don standing beside it. No one knew just what to say. Don was the first to break the silence.

"I guess it was foolish," he said a little shamefacedly.

It had been foolish, in so far as the automobile headlight had been concerned. Later he admitted that it had been very little help in landing. He could have done almost as well without it. Luck, skill, and his flying "instinct" had had more to do with that first landing than what someone in the crowd referred to as "Don's bicycle lamp."

This trial-and-error experiment had shown one thing. A stronger light was necessary. If this was a questionable contribution to the solution of the problem of night flying, it did not discourage Bruner, even though at that time he could not manage to find a stronger light. Instead, his next experiments were devoted to altering the position of the light on the plane and trying to find out where it was most effective. Along the wings, from tip to tip, he tried almost every possible position for the light. He even experimented with it on the tail of the plane. In each position the light was tested in actual flight.

The difficulties Bruner faced were enormous. There was no enlisted personnel available to help him at night. He had to depend on the volunteer services of civilians, most of whom were impelled by curiosity. But there was one civilian who was more than curious. He believed that Bruner was on the track of something real. This was an engineer named Carpenter, who became Don's faithful ally to such an extent that he put his life in jeopardy by accompanying Bruner on most of his flights.

Some of these flights were made under anything but favorable conditions. There were times when forced landings had to be made. Others when the light itself would be almost shaken loose by the vibrations of the engine. The supply of gasoline allowed for these experiments was small, and always had to be considered. Don himself refers to those early flights as "just stumbling around in the dark."

But the flights went on. Some advance was made when Don, through the nuisance value of his persistence, finally persuaded the authorities to allow him to use a special lamp built experimentally for motion-picture projection. This lamp, mounted in a streamlined case, was a big improvement over the old headlight, but it was not until electric generators were installed on the Liberty engine and the candle power of the light could be materially increased, that real headway was made.

By this time most of the skeptics had been convinced. The ridicule was replaced by genuine interest as Bruner's experiments, even with makeshift and inadequate equipment, began to show that the thing he was striving for, far from being an impossible dream, was practical. Those who had lacked the imagination to visualize Bruner's aims soon began to see the increasingly successful results of his experiments.

Gradually the lamp began to take shape. Working with the concentrated filament type lamp used in motion-picture projectors, and aided finally by a generator to give him the necessary increase in current supply and candle power, Bruner made two wingtip lamps enclosed in bullet-shaped casings that looked like large-caliber artillery shells. A mirrored, parabolic reflector was incorporated to concentrate the beam of light, and definite progress was immediately apparent. Another experiment called for a smaller, powerful light mounted on a swivel on the fuselage of a Martin bomber, in a manner similar to the present-day automobile spotlights that are mounted next the windshield.

At the end of four years of hard, dangerous work during which over two thousand night flights were made, Lieutenant Bruner finally developed the airplane landing lamp which, without any basic changes, has become part of the standard equipment of most aircraft built in the United States.

The main purpose of these lamps, contrary to popular belief, is not so much to reveal or light up the landing field, which a flare dropped from two or three thousand feet will do, but to show clearly any obstructions on the field that might wreck the plane while it is still rolling along the ground. The flare, casting its unearthly magnesium glare from high in the air, will show the position of the field itself, and any major obstacles such as trees, power lines, etc. But this "flat" overhead lighting is deceptive. From the air, as he circles down on the field, the pilot cannot judge relative heights of smaller obstructions. Often he cannot see at all such things as ditches, boulders, or other obstacles that might crack up a ship landing at high speed. But the brilliant beams from Bruner's perfected lights, streaming from the front of the plane, as an automobile headlight beam streams ahead of the car, can pick out far ahead and in sharp relief every tiny bump and depression. And this is necessary, even in lighted fields.

To just what extent the vision of the "dreamer" Bruner

was justified was seen in 1923, when Don had the satisfaction of being summoned to headquarters at McCook Field to meet officials of the United States Post Office Department. They had been following Bruner's experiments to make night flying safe and practical, and now they had come to ask advice on the establishment of night air-mail service, as well as to have one of their own planes equipped with his landing lights which had by then been adopted by the Army.

Here was vindication of his theories. Commercial night flying was about to be established. Little wonder then if Lieutenant—First Lieutenant by now—Bruner felt a thrill of pride which did much to erase the memory of disappointment and hardship that are the birth pangs of every significant contribution to the progress of man.

About this time, too, the General Electric Company became interested in his work, and sent illumination engineers to work with Bruner. With their added resources and equipment, the lights were brought to an even higher state of utility and perfection. Air-mail planes were equipped with them, and from a foolhardy project night flying rapidly became the accepted thing. Another milestone was passed in aviation's progress.

Bruner's contributions to night flying did not cease with the perfection of landing lights. During his night flights in Texas he had noted that the large, bright electric signs in cities made excellent guides. With this idea in mind, he experimented with various lights and evolved the rotating searchlight, essentially as it exists today. His idea of marking air routes with beacons was also adopted, and transport pilots on all commercial air routes from coast to coast are guided today in part by these winking eyes.

He developed and perfected floodlights for landing fields and lighted wind cones to show the direction the wind was blowing. He worked out airport light systems employing a color code: white lights to mark the limits of the field, red lights to indicate obstacles such as overhead wires and buildings, green lights to indicate the best approaches . . . all things so familiar today that they are taken for granted, but in the beginning developments of the early dreams of Don Bruner.

One unfamiliar with airplanes might hardly notice the "eyes" set so unobtrusively in the huge modern planes of today, two curved glass surfaces in the leading edge of the wing equidistant from the ship's center, their highly polished reflectors catching and reflecting the daylight with a fixed stare, and coming to life at night with a fierce, steady beam. And watching those lights, set like the eyes in a Chinese junk, one would scarcely be apt to realize that a tremendous part of present-day commercial aviation could not exist without them. For, as the Chinese say of the eyes painted on their boats, "A boat with no eyes cannot see where to go," so can we say, of night-flying commercial planes, without lights they could not see where to land and the indispensable twenty-four-hour service of transport ships might still be a dream of the future.

Don Bruner was commissioned Captain in 1931, a rank he retained until his retirement in 1933 for disability incurred in the line of duty. Unspectacular, without cheering crowds to spur him on, he led a career that involved hazardous, difficult work. Had he failed there would have been no glory . . . only one more charred and smoking wreck on a dark and lonely airfield. His courage was selfless, of the same high order as the scientist who, in a remote laboratory, works with dangerous disease toxin in order to test a new serum. His pledge, made twenty years ago on a Texas field, was more than redeemed. And his achievement stands forth even in the undramatic and terse language of the Army citation, when he was awarded the Distinguished Flying Cross shortly before his retirement:

". . . For extraordinary achievement while participating in aerial flights. By his vision, initiative, courage, and perseverance, Captain Bruner rendered exceptionally valuable services to the Government of the United States by developing and perfecting night flying equipment, thus making it possible for military and commercial airplanes to traverse the length and breadth of the United States during the hours of darkness."

Chapter 5

FLYING FORMULAS

Alexander Klemin

Back in the year 1902 an earnest young man with a bushy head of hair headed a debate. The place was a preparatory school in London where he was a student fitting himself to take up engineering, and the subject of the debate was: "Resolved, that flight in a heavier-than-air machine is impossible." Alexander Klemin, the embryo electrical engineer, took the affirmative, defending the belief of Simon Newcomb that man would never fly without a gas bag to support him. Supported by all the science and mathematics at his command, he proved to his own satisfaction that heavier-than-air flight was impossible and, incidentally, won the debate. His point proved, young Klemin promptly considered the matter closed and went on with his studies.

Even when the Wrights made history a year later at Kitty Hawk and aviation struggled along in its primitive beginnings the subject remained, to Klemin, still closed.

In the middle '30's if one were inspecting the University Heights division of New York University he would find the building of the Daniel Guggenheim School of Aeronautics, one of the foremost institutions of its kind in the world, its façade unimposing, its entrance chastely Roman. Within, he would find walls of rough building tile and corridors of cement. He would open doors to busy laboratories filled with instruments, engines, and plane parts, bustling with grease-smudged young men and clamorous with the noises of active experimentation. In the heart of the building, in an office lined to the ceiling with books and piled with a vast accumulation of scientific data, he would find one of the founders and prime movers of the Guggenheim School—its Director, Doctor Alexander Klemin. The same man who, thirty-odd years previously, had so staunchly proved the impossibility of heavier-than-air flight and then forgotten it.

The mass of hair would be the same, though gray-shot, and Klemin, with a quarter century of aviation pioneering behind him, would present the same combination of scientific accuracy and assurance that marked the young engineering student. He would insist, too, though with a slightly saturnine gleam of humor in his eyes, that in the light of then existing knowledge and engines he was correct in the debate.

By the time Alex Klemin had graduated from London University as an electrical engineer, man had flown and was continuing to fly, if erratically and somewhat dangerously. This bothered Klemin not at all. It failed, indeed, to interest him particularly. When aviation again came into his ken it was as a mathematical problem.

Young Klemin became known among his friends as a wizard at applied mechanics and one day in 1910 a young man of his acquaintance approached him, seeking help.

"Look," said the young man frantically, "these new regulations of the British Admiralty have got me in a tangle. I've got to have a week's work in aeronautical stress calculations done by Monday." This was on Friday.

"Why come to me?" Klemin inquired.

"Because," was the answer, "I can't get them out alone—and if I don't, I'll get the sack."

That was something else again. Klemin pitched in with characteristic energy upon this purely mathematical job, as a favor to his friend. All Friday night the two men worked, and all Saturday and Sunday, brewing gallons of black coffee and bluing the air with cigarette smoke. Monday morning found the job completed.

Two results accrued from this. The young man kept his job and Klemin, who had never so much as seen a flight, or sat in the rickety crates of the time, found aviation design so fascinating that he determined he would be one of its engineers. True, eight years before he had conclusively proved the impossibility of building powered aircraft that would fly, but Klemin found no contradiction in this. Here was a new science, an unexplored field with huge quantities of work to be done, hundreds of equations to be worked out, reams of paper to be scribbled with formulas. And Klemin was never quite so happy as when surrounded by paper scraps scribbled with calculations in heavy black pencil.

Forget, for the moment, today's flying giants, transcontinental airways, radio beams, and transatlantic flights. When Klemin became interested, flying was a daredevil's game. Men went up in flimsy contraptions of bamboo and ash and cloth, sitting precariously on the wing, never knowing when a stray gust of wind might send their craft crashing to earth. Crowds gathered to watch each flight with curiosity not unmixed with awe and the morbid expectation of seeing a fatal crackup. All too often their hopes were rewarded. Flying was done at an average height of fifty feet. One hundred feet was considered real altitude. And plane construction was almost wholly a matter of trial and error. The pilot figured his plane was all right if he emerged from the first flight alive.

Klemin tells about it with a certain grim and mischievous relish. The same sly humor that so oddly offsets his professorial façade glints in his eye as he tells about the arguments long ago over whether a ship should have a lifting tail or a nonlifting tail.

"The battle raged pro and con," he chuckled reminiscently. "I was opposed to the lifting tail. And there was one unanswerable argument, then, to back me up. Every man who went up in a ship with a lifting tail was killed!" But Klemin felt no callousness for the daring men who lost their lives, rather an impersonal and mischievous amusement over a point proved which was quite apart from personal or emotional considerations.

In pursuit of his goal, aeronautical engineering, young Klemin read exhaustively on dynamics, hydrodynamics, and other recondite branches of aeronautics. Then one day in South Kensington Library he happened to glance over the shoulder of a man thoroughly disreputable-looking, his collar tattered and frayed, half the buttons off his waistcoat, fingernails black, and hands grubby. What attracted Klemin was the fact that the man was reading one of Lagrange's early contributions to analytical mechanics, a highly abstruse work on mathematics.

Klemin spoke to him and found that he was a Third Wangler, one of the highest mathematical distinctions obtainable. Because of his personal habits and an abominable stammer he had been fired from every teaching job he ever held, in spite of an amazing knowledge of advanced mathematics. Klemin immediately engaged him as a tutor.

"He was a good teacher for me," Klemin says, "because he couldn't really explain anything. I had to dig down for myself in order to understand him." But he did teach Klemin more mathematics than most engineers ever know.

About a year later, Klemin came to America and enrolled at Massachusetts Institute of Technology as the first student in Jerome C. Hunsaker's newly organized aero engineering course. His progress at M. I. T. was so rapid and his ability so marked that when Hunsaker left the school to head the new Aircraft Division in Washington young Klemin was invited to succeed him as chief of the M. I. T. aeronautics department. In a speech at his installation, Professor Peabody expressed "regrets" for the Institute at having to take on so young a man for so important a position. Though it was to a great extent professorial facetiousness, there was real alarm at the idea of putting so young a man in so responsible a position.

"And," says Doctor Klemin gleefully, "they made no bones about informing me that the only reason they did so was because there was no older man who was equipped to be Hunsaker's successor."

Klemin plunged into his work with gusto, and the faculty never found reason to regret its decision. At this time Lester D. Gardner asked Klemin to collaborate in founding a really technical aeronautical magazine. There was no such publication in America at the time and Klemin added this job to his very full schedule. As Technical Editor of the magazine he toured the country with Gardner, visiting plant after plant and conferring with the foremost constructors of the day. Out of the trip came one of the most important features of the new magazine.

Aviation, as it was called, presented in its first issue the beginning of a full course in aeronautics and airplane design, giving for the first time in the English language a complete and systematic presentation of the subject in such a way as to be of maximum value to the constructor and designer. Klemin and Gardner had made available a reference text giving full details for imposing loads on the structure of planes, showing how to use the principles of applied mechanics in calculations for various plane parts, and making clear the fundamental aerodynamic principles of airplane construction.

The course was an instantaneous success and was immediately adopted as a standard text by Army and Navy instructors. Its influence on the engineering side of aviation was enormous, and no one can gauge how many lives it helped to save, or just how much it furthered the cause of American aviation.

When the war broke out Klemin was recommended for a commission in the Army Air Service. In an interview with the Chief of Personnel there were certain differences of opinion, and Klemin, with a characteristic brashness, saw no reason to temper his remarks with diplomacy. The net result was that Klemin did not receive his Majority. But since Colonel V. E. Clark, commanding officer at McCook Field and another former Hunsaker pupil, needed him urgently, Klemin joined the Army and, as a sergeant, went to McCook Field. He was in the oddly anomalous position of being a noncommissioned officer, yet in full charge of the research department and reputedly knowing more of aerodynamics than anyone else at the field.

Telling about it, Klemin takes a half-chewed cigar from his mouth and settles back in satisfied recollection in his chair.

"I was in a beautiful position of irresponsibility," he says. "I was in full charge of research and free to go on with my work at the field, yet so low in rank that I made a poor target for reorganization or demotion."

He did have pretty much his own way—which meant he got things done with a minimum of Army red tape. He wanted to learn to fly—to add to his theoretical knowledge of aviation. But there was no flying instruction being given at McCook Field. So Sergeant Klemin issued orders to himself to conduct observation flights on a number of ships! He taught Al and Jimmie Johnson the theory of flight, while they taught him to handle the controls. The results were almost disastrous to all parties concerned. The Johnsons couldn't learn the theory of flight, while Klemin had a tendency to be naturally heavy-handed at the controls. His peculiar antics in the air were a source of never-ending delight to the McCook personnel. For hours, while in the air with the Johnsons, Klemin would launch into arguments and discussions, shouting over the noise of the motors, attempting to co-ordinate theory with practice. And it would wind up with his taking the stick and nearly cracking up the ship.

In addition to learning to fly after a fashion, Klemin did much more. His work at McCook Field, particularly his contributions to the stress analysis of airplanes, was of far-reaching importance. There remained at that time considerable uncertainty as to the strength of an airplane, even after all calculations had been made. While to an engineer it represented a problem to be worked out on paper, to a flier defects in a new plane often meant the difference between life and death.

Sergeant Klemin viewed the current method of sand-testing with a stern and disapproving eye. It was more a matter of discipline than of science. Privates, in very military maneuvers, marched smartly to the plane being tested, halted, placed a sandbag on a wing, wheeled sharply, and marched away, repeating the maneuver until the approximate load had been placed on the plane.

Sergeant Klemin had been requested to work with a French aviation mission which had come to McCook Field to help the United States in the technical problems of aviation. Europe, then having three years of war flying behind her, was far in advance of America. Together, Klemin and the French worked out a set of specifications for the load factors and for the distribution of the loads along the wing span. Realizing that the wings in flight are supported by the pull of air on their *upper* surfaces they applied the method which Hunsaker and Zahm had observed in a British laboratory before the war. The plane was mounted upside down for sand-testing, and the weight applied in a direction to simulate stressing of the wings in flight.

Klemin recruited enlisted men from the field, trained them, and made sand-testing a customary scientific safety measure that indubitably saved the lives of many American fliers.

American industry, under war contracts, had begun making the English De Havilland-4, known familiarly as the DH-4. A more powerful motor—the famed Liberty motor of American design—was substituted for the original British engine, and on the first vibration test Klemin's method disclosed that a slight modification in the attachment of certain bracing wires had reduced the strength at one point to a dangerous degree. Other defects, too, were discovered and remedied without the necessity for fatal crashes to bring them to light.

Test flights were haphazard affairs compared to those of today. The best instruments gave no reliable indication of the actual speed of a plane. Climb calculations were made without allowance for varying atmospheric pressure. So Klemin, with the help of the French mission and some English publications, established and wrote up full specifications for flight testing. All data were supplied, instruments to be used were described, methods of correction and calculation were specified, to give as accurate results as possible. For the first time in America, speed tests were made in both directions to eliminate the errors caused by a head wind or a tail wind. Results were reduced to a "standard atmosphere" and instruments were properly calibrated. This set a basis for flight performance testing which remains today basically unaltered.

Klemin had meanwhile been promoted to a Lieutenancy. Still his work was not entirely under ideal conditions. Army red tape wound itself more than once about his short, stocky figure. His habit of saying flatly what he felt to be true sometimes produced complications because he ignored often the very real necessity for tact.

On one occasion a civilian brought to the field some 125 wing sections. He had, on the authority of the General, permission to monopolize the wind tunnel to test them. Klemin took one look at the sections, saw immediately that they were warped to the point of worthlessness, and said, "No." There was no point in tying up the busy wind tunnel.

"But I have direct orders from the General," the civilian protested. Klemin's hair bristled and his eyes snapped angrily. "What the hell does the General know about wings!" he roared.

On the basis of that unmilitary remark a warrant was sworn out against Klemin charging him with a variety of startling military crimes. An investigation was ordered.

The affair might have had a very unfortunate ending except that the investigator turned out to be a former student of Klemin's who had since become a Major in the Air Service. The case was successively stalled along until the Armistice came, and ultimately the whole matter was dropped.

After the war, Klemin entered into private practice as a consulting aeronautical engineer. Many design competitions at that time were won by ships of his design. He became consulting engineer to the government in the inauguration of the United States Air Mail Service, and he developed the first amphibian gear ever to be employed in American aviation.

Also about this time, Klemin gave an elective course in aeronautics at New York University which so aroused the interest of the students that Dean Collins P. Bliss of the College of Engineering invited him to undertake a full course in aeronautics. Only after Klemin accepted the appointment did it turn out that there was no money available for the new course. It was through Alex Klemin's many friends in the aviation industry that the course was financed and N. Y. U. was able to carry through its first effort in aeronautical instruction.

Professor Klemin now had something to sink his teeth into. His first course began at N. Y. U. in 1923–24. Only seven or eight students were enrolled, and there was practically no equipment, not even a room. Klemin thrust a cigar between his teeth, marshaled his class in a corner of the transformer room amidst a litter of electrical equipment, and taught the entire course by himself. In June every man granted a degree found placement in the aviation industry.

In the second year the Curtiss Airplane and Motor Corporation built a new, large wind tunnel and donated the old four-foot one to N. Y. U. This helped to make the instruction more practical. When the second graduating class in its entirety found positions in the industry, Dean Bliss agreed that aeronautics should be placed upon an enlarged and more permanent basis. Klemin went to every effort to organize a committee that would secure the necessary funds. One day he persuaded Harry F. Guggenheim, a former naval flier, to attend a meeting. This resulted in Harry's father, Daniel Guggenheim, endowing the school with $500,000 for the purpose of training engineers who could do the practical, necessary job of designing, building, and developing aircraft and engines on a scientific basis.

While the building for the Guggenheim School was being erected Klemin also worked out with Harry Guggenheim a plan for an additional Fund for the Promotion of Aeronautics. This was endowed by Daniel Guggenheim to the extent of $2,500,000. One of the outstanding achievements of this fund was the establishment of the Guggenheim Safe Aircraft Competition, which was to improve the landing speed, landing run, take-off run, "getaway," and control at the stall. Klemin prepared the first draft of the rules, and the necessary equipment for the tests was collected and calibrated at the laboratories of the Guggenheim School.

The Safe Aircraft Competition marked an important era in American aviation. Another significant aspect of the work done by the fund was the endowment of a number of other schools of aeronautics in America. The establishment of these schools greatly aided the transfer of the center of aerodynamical research from Europe to America after the First World War. The blind landing experiments made by Lieutenant James Doolittle under the auspices of the fund were the first steps taken in reducing the terrors of fog-bound landings for fliers. The fund's experimental weather service pointed the way to the necessity for the present complete weather service to all the airlines of the United States.

Doctor Klemin, with his varied interests in aviation, also found time to write many books on aviation, including *Airplane Stress Analysis, Simplified Aerodynamics*, and *If You Want to Fly*.

Though not the sentimental type in the least, Doctor Klemin nevertheless "fathered" many students who passed through the Guggenheim School, and constantly acted as a benevolent employment agent for them. Old students continually come back to see him, consult with him, or give him news about their lives and careers. He growls that whenever he sees an old student he expects to cough up with a job, a wedding present, or a gift for a new baby, but he undoubtedly loves it.

In his laboratory he would seem at times like a rumple-haired Einstein with a deep and impersonal abstraction and again like a mischievous lad playing pranks among the balances and scales of the wind tunnels, taking time out for a laugh at himself. At lunch he might, for no apparent reason, launch into a long, detailed explanation of some problem, covering the tablecloth with formulas, hieroglyphics, and diagrams comprehensible only to himself. Actually, he would be busy convincing himself of some point, while letting his lunch get cold. He could never say more than a few words without scribbling symbols in heavy black pencil on paper. On his lighter side, he invented a game of three-dimensional checkers for the amusement of his young daughter, Diana. It is played much the same as ordinary checkers, except that there are two planes of checkers, one above the other.

Klemin's younger associates in the department always worked wholeheartedly with him, and the Guggenheim School, under his direction, has perhaps done more than any other single agency to assure American aviation its preeminent place in the world.

Although he flew in all sorts of rickety "crates," his only accident occurred when the foundation for the Guggenheim School was being excavated. Klemin fell into a trench, breaking his leg in eight places. Newspapers reported erroneously that he had fallen thousands of feet in a plane.

One near accident is indicative of the fact that without being a professional flier he always had something of the flier's attitude rather than the cautious professor's. Back in the days at McCook Field one ship had some loosened wires that vibrated badly. In the interests of safety Klemin ordered the ship grounded. Someone tauntingly asked, "What's the matter—are you afraid to fly in it?"

Klemin went up immediately in the plane. As he landed one of the wires broke and wound itself about the propeller. He had narrowly escaped a fatal crash. Klemin grinned triumphantly as he emerged. "Now do you believe me?"

He would probably have been delighted—if not killed— if the ship *had* crashed to prove his point.

Chapter 6

OL' EAGLE EYE

Albert W. Stevens

On the third of March 1929, the nation's capital, after the busy preparations for the inauguration of President Hoover on the following day, lay quietly sleeping. Over the White House the sound of an airplane motor grew to an angry drone, a loud roar. Then a dazzling blaze of light and a tremendous explosion awakened the neighborhood. Panes of glass tinkled from the concussion. Shortly, a similar flashing crash shook the Capitol. Surprise and consternation reigned until it was determined that an air raid was not in progress. Captain Albert W. Stevens was merely taking night photographs of the Capitol and White House with flash bombs.

Stevens had arranged it as a "stunt," although not with the idea of shocking the public or of gaining personal publicity. It was "Steve's" characteristic and rather dramatic way of reminding official Washington that there was an Air Corps, and particularly an Aerial Photography Division. The thought that persons might be startled or windows broken hadn't occurred to him. As always, his interest lay entirely in his beloved photography.

For his first three hours' flying that night Stevens had only torn and bleeding fingers to show for his labors. They were the result of frantic efforts to dislodge a flash bomb that had become wedged in the bomb rack.

The bleeding-finger episode was one of a series of unlucky incidents in this exploit. The venture began at half past seven in the evening when Captain Stevens, accompanied by Lieutenant John D. Corkille, took off in a standard Douglas O2 observation plane. The plane was equipped for night flying with landing lights and long exhaust stacks to conceal the exhaust flames, which would otherwise obscure the vision of those in the airplane as well as fog the film. In order not to create too great a disturbance in the vicinity, Stevens reduced the usual charge of magnesium powder in the flash bomb, with the result that the photograph of the White House was underexposed. When the plane was flown over the Capitol the bomb rack failed to function, and the bomb stuck tight in spite of Captain Stevens's effort to extricate it with his fingers. Since no photograph of the Capitol could be made, Corkille flew the plane back to Bolling Field where bombs of larger capacity were procured, and another effort was made to get pictures of the Capitol. The explosion of the first bomb was so great that it shattered glass in nearby windows, but the photograph obtained was sharp and clear. Then further misfortune interfered. An attempt to get another photo-

graph of the Capitol failed. A part of the Captain's parachute, which every Army aviator must wear, got tangled
up in some way or other with the electric switch so that
when the flash bomb was released the shutter of the camera
failed to trip. Despite these tribulations, Captain Stevens
developed the negatives while the plane was circling aloft
over the Potomac and dropped them to the ground at a
prearranged spot, where they were to be relayed to the
office of the telegraph company. But this plan worked
badly, too. Captain Stevens's aim was good, for the bag
dropped within ten feet of the officers who were waiting
for it. But the red flare which had been attached to it blew
out, and the officers could not see where it had landed.
Trees and shrubbery dotted the ground and darkness made
further search seem futile. The exasperated searchers finally
phoned Bolling Field, to which Captain Stevens had returned by this time, and told him of their failure to find the
precious negatives. Then Stevens justified his nickname of
Ol' Eagle Eye. "The bag dropped," he said, "close to the
wire fence, and within thirty feet of the gate." Hastening
to the spot indicated, they found the bag hanging on the
fence he had mentioned. Speeding through the air, high
above the dark field, Ol' Eagle Eye had had the point exactly located.

The films were rushed to the telegraph office and tele-
photos were sent to various distant points for press use as
part of the stunt. At the cost of disturbing, unintentionally,
the sleep of the nation's outgoing president, Calvin Coolidge, in his last night in the White House, Stevens by this

noisy experiment had dramatized the practicability of taking night photographs, developing them in the air, and dropping the pictures made on a special film, all in the course of a few minutes.

This demonstration was only one, of the minor achievements in the work-filled career of Captain Stevens. A member of the old McCook Field group, and one who later worked on the same site when it became known as Wright Field, Captain Stevens more than any other individual is responsible for pioneering the present highly developed science of aerial photography. Its value is more than a military one, though that in itself would justify the years of experiment. For tax assessments, contour mapping, soil erosion control, hydroelectric power developments, forest conservation, harbor improvements—these and a thousand other uses make the aerial camera of today an invaluable aid to technological and agricultural progress. A photographic plane can make accurate contour maps of a region in a matter of hours or days, while the same information obtained by pack-mule and transit requires weeks and months at many times the cost.

Taking pictures from the air requires a high degree of skill, born of years of experience. It calls for aeronautical skill and knowledge of flying, photographic chemistry, optics, engineering, and a host of other highly specialized fields. There were few men who possessed this combination of special knowledge in the early '20's. Daring, too, was a requisite when flying over tropical jungle or jagged mountain peaks hundreds of miles from any landing field, beacon, or aerial guidepost—or when climbing into the sub-zero of the stratosphere and risking freezing and suffocation. The tremendous patience to make thousands of exposures, develop thousands of films on a single expedition, and the tremendous enthusiasm for photography and the air—all these attributes were combined in a single, genial, keen-eyed Army officer who helped make photographic history.

Albert Stevens's interest in photography started in the early nineteen-hundreds while he was a student at the University of Maine, working for a degree in science. Long before graduation young Stevens needed money to continue his course. He earned it by doing newspaper work and by selling photographs for commercial use. An enthusiastic amateur photographer, Stevens soon became adept. By the time he graduated, he had as much photographic knowledge as any professional photographer. But as yet he made no use of this ability.

In 1907 he received his B. S. and in 1908 his Master's degree. Then, for nine years, he knocked about the country as an engineer, first as an electrical engineer in charge of various water-power plants throughout the United States, later as engineer-in-charge of gold-mining operations in Idaho and Alaska. In Alaska his experiences awakened old longings for adventure, though his duties themselves involved more adventure than many men ever experience. He made long winter journeys into the interior, by dog sled, with only Eskimos for company, and many times, when overtaken by howling Arctic blizzards, sought shelter in the snow huts of the natives. On many of those long, cold nights spent in semi-darkness, with walrus meat for breakfast, dinner, and supper, young Stevens's fancy left the odorous, gloomy hut and his thoughts went back to boyhood days in Belfast, Maine, as he wandered along the docks to watch the ships come in, or looked out over the bay, hopeful of the day he might cross the Atlantic. That was one dream that was not realized until the World War took him overseas.

It was in January 1918 at the age of thirty-one that Albert Stevens enlisted in the Aviation Section of the Signal Reserve Corps. His superiors were quick to note that for all his enthusiasm and ability in aviation his capabilities as a photographer were exceptional. Less than two months after enlistment he was commissioned a first lieutenant and assigned to duty in the School of Aerial Photography at Cornell University. After a short, intensive course of study he was placed in command of the Sixth Photo Section and sent overseas.

His work with the American Expeditionary Force in Europe, taking photos of enemy positions while flying over their lines, was as short in duration as it was daring in execution and brilliant in accomplishment. In the brief time between his first flight overseas in July and the Armistice in November he received two citations. Just before the Armistice he was appointed Chief Photographic Officer of the Air Service with the First Army.

Important and valuable as his wartime work was during those last decisive months on the Western Front, his real work had only just begun. When hostilities were over he gave serious thought to phases of his subject which he had been compelled to ignore under combat conditions. Many times during the war he had thought on the possibilities of an improved technique in aerial photography. Now, with no "Archie" bursts under him or enemy machine guns peppering him, he could begin devising those methods which today by mathematical formulas make possible exact plotting of artillery range on an enemy position after photographs have been made. It meant that in the future no position would be invulnerable if a camera plane could cover it and return the information to its own command. The click of an aerial camera's shutter thus came to be feared as much as the dropping of a bomb.

The following February, Stevens was commissioned Captain. He remained in France until August 1919, then returned to America, where he was assigned to duty in the office of the Chief of the Air Service in Washington. Later he served for a short time at Langley Field, and finally went to McCook Field, which became the center of his operations.

Once settled at McCook Field, Captain Stevens plunged zestfully into the work at hand. There were new methods of plotting and mapping to be worked out, new cameras to be developed, and experiments in high-altitude photography to be made. As Chief of the Aerial Photographic Unit, Materiel Division, Steve, as his friends called him, was in an ideal spot, exactly the right man for the job he loved. Never did enthusiastic amateur ride a hobby with

more enthusiasm than Stevens did his job. Yet, with his
voracious appetite for work and more work, Stevens never
became a mere automaton. He was among the most popular officers at the field, modest and generous to a fault, a
man's man. When he received praise for some exceptional bit of work he would invariably answer, "If I didn't
have Corkille I'd never have made it at all," and he would
gesture to Lieutenant John D. Corkille, one of the Air
Corps' best pilots and the favorite teammate of Stevens.
Or again, he would say, "If I hadn't had a good plane and
engine, it would have been just too bad for Stevie."

Aerial photography is, after all, a highly specialized and
exacting job, with many variable problems to interfere
with the securing of a good picture. The plane must be
held steady and level when shooting, which is why Stevens
valued Corkille as a pilot so highly. There are conditions of
haze in long-distance work not found in simple ground
camera work, and there is need for extreme accuracy in
map-making photography. Grueling hours of flying and
darkroom work were taken in Captain Stevens's stride as
experiments with various film emulsions, filters, and new
cameras went on.

In September 1928, Captain Stevens took off, with
Lieutenant Jimmy Doolittle as pilot, in the same plane used
by Lieutenant Macready in making his world's altitude
record in 1927. The purpose of the flight was to test photographic and other high-altitude equipment.

For an hour and twenty-five minutes the plane climbed
steadily until at the maximum altitude a temperature of

fifty-seven degrees below zero Centigrade was registered (70.6 below zero Fahrenheit). Their clock froze up, as well as one of the spirit levels on Stevens's camera, and Doolittle found the controls difficult to operate because of the intense cold. The oxygen supply proved to be insufficient for two persons. After making some eighteen exposures, Captain Stevens temporarily lost consciousness while Doolittle became semi-unconscious just before turning the nose of the plane downward.

Descent took only forty-five minutes, with both men recovering as lower altitudes were reached. When the plane landed the camera was covered with ice and a spot on Stevens's cheek was frozen. In spite of a scattering of clouds at 6000 feet, his photographs showed highways and outstanding structures beneath with remarkable clarity. The pictures were so sharp that they could be enlarged ten diameters. Thirty-three square miles were covered by the exposures. These were photos that in wartime would have been of inestimable value.

On this occasion, however, the pictures served a new purpose. The computation of altitude in feet or meters has always been on a more or less theoretical basis. Barograph (recording altimeter) records are taken, and from a fixed formula in which average temperatures are arbitrarily assumed for the various altitudes the height is worked out. This method, adopted by the Fédération Aéronautique Internationale, is not necessarily accurate according to a tape-line measure, but since it is obviously impossible to drop a tape-line down some thirty or forty thousand feet this system gave as accurate a reckoning as possible, using the knowledge at hand.

However, the photos made by Stevens on his flight with Doolittle were to be used for a new method of computing the altitude above ground. If three or more points on the ground are selected, with the distances between them known from accurate ground survey data, and if the focal length of the lens (distance from the film to the optical center of the lens) is known, the distance between the points can be measured on the picture. The problem becomes a simple geometrical one of similar triangles, and can be mathematically computed to within one-tenth of one per cent.

This photographic method was not intended to supplant the standard F. A. I. system but was to serve as a positive check against existing methods to determine their relative accuracy.

Unfortunately on this first flight the two barographs taken along failed to function and it was not possible to make the comparison. The flight revealed many important features, nonetheless: the need for a better oxygen supply, the efficiency of electrically heated goggles, and the need for heating devices on instruments and camera to prevent frosting over at sub-zero temperatures. Small electric heaters were applied to the clock and camera, and heating units were fitted to the leather flying mittens worn by the aviators. In December Stevens made another flight with Lieutenant Harry A. Johnson as pilot, reaching an altitude of 36,903 feet, computed by F. A. I. standards. When calculated by the photo measurement system it was nearer 39,000 feet, breaking Stevens's own previous record.

In February 1929, Stevens made another record flight and secured superb pictures, again with Johnson as pilot. This flight, as well as the night photographing of the Capitol in March, was mentioned in the awarding of the Mackay Trophy for 1929 to Stevens. A third achievement mentioned in the Mackay Trophy award was Stevens's famous photograph of Mount Rainier from a distance of 227 miles. This widely acclaimed photo was made during Captain Stevens's 14,000-mile photographic tour of the Northwest with Lieutenant Corkille, who acted as pilot. The project was authorized by the War Department because of the valuable contributions to military photography it was expected to bring, and results exceeded expectations. Supersensitive panchromatic film emulsions were being newly developed, and using a Kryptocyanine sensitized film with a red filter, Captain Stevens made a photo above Crater Lake in southern Oregon at an altitude of 17,000 feet that clearly showed Mount Rainier, 227 miles distant.

Haze ordinarily limits human vision to about twenty-seven miles, and has a corresponding effect upon a photographic emulsion because the latter is particularly sensitive to blue and ultraviolet rays. The diffusion of these rays by vapor and dust creates an impenetrable haze. But in making this photo, Stevens used the then new infrared film, covering the camera lens with a deep red filter which "strained out" all the blue and violet rays and admitted the longer infrared rays, invisible to the eye. The landmarks he was photographing were invisible to Ol' Eagle Eye, hovering 17,000 feet up. But consulting his compass he pointed his camera in the direction of Mount Rainier and made the exposure. When the film was developed the Three Sisters Mountains were shown in the foreground, while successively in the distance loomed Mount Washington, Three-Fingered Jack, Mount Jefferson, Mount Hood, Mount Saint Helena, and Mount Rainier. Mount Rainier appeared lower than the other peaks because of the curvature of the earth, plainly visible in the photo. When the distance on the map was measured it was found to be 227 miles from the camera plane, a new long-distance record for photographs. This record Stevens himself exceeded in 1932 by a similar photograph during a California mapping project. Piloted by Lieutenant J. F. Phillips, Captain Stevens from a point eight miles east of Salinas, California, and at an altitude of 23,000 feet successfully photographed Mount Shasta 331.2 miles from the camera. Here, too, the photo was made by dead reckoning on an invisible objective and an area was covered that, but for the curvature of the earth, would have included 26,000 square miles! However, the earth's curvature foreshortened, necessarily, the distant part of the picture. Plainly shown were the Santa Cruz Mountains, the Santa Clara Valley, and Sacramento Valley, an area of 7200 square miles. Reference to the reproduced photo makes this clear.

Never content to rest upon his laurels, Stevens went to work at McCook on a new five-lens aerial camera on the lines of one designed by Major Bagley that had three lenses. This instrument, which was used in conjunction with a special printing machine, had an unusually wide angle of view and was constructed with a precision never before used. Its advantage was that it gave an extreme wide-angle view without the distortion of a very wide-angle lens, which could not be used for the accurate job of mapmaking. The lenses were so mounted that one faced vertically downward, while the other four were at oblique angles. From the five-part negative the special transforming printer projected the four oblique photos into the same plane as the vertical one, giving a finished picture, undistorted, of exceptionally wide angle of view.

This camera was tested on a mapping survey of New England. A total of 3600 square miles was covered in *two flying days*, an area which would have taken half a year to map with ordinary equipment. The entire project was done at high altitudes. Fifteen flying hours were spent at 20,000 feet. Oxygen was used, and the improved equipment eliminated the usual physiological reactions of nausea and headache. At 20,000 feet the camera covered an area twenty miles wide, while the length of the "strips" photographed was seventy-five miles. Eight hundred negatives were made, slightly overlapping laterally, and overlapping fifty-five per cent in the direction of flight. On this flight a new, supersensitive panchromatic film was used, as well as a new infrared film, then being experimentally developed by Eastman Laboratories. The infrared film was twice as fast as previous similar films and was exposed through a filter passing only invisible infrared rays—a filter which, to the eye, seemed quite black and opaque.

The value of this research for peace as well as war was enormous. It permitted accurate mapping at one-thirtieth the cost and a small fraction of the time consumed in ground surveys. This and similar mapping expeditions furnished the basis for the later work undertaken by Fairchild Aerial Surveys. The New England project was done for the United States Geological Survey under the Department of the Interior, which reimbursed the Air Corps for the cost of the work.

That project, too, probably recalled to Stevens his first postwar mapping job in the White Mountains, sponsored by the Army Air Corps in collaboration with the Fairchild Camera Company and designed to test one of the first multi-lensed cameras. The territory was a virgin one so far as aircraft were concerned, for no Army plane had ever been farther north in New England than Concord, New Hampshire. It was a mountainous forest country without landing fields or beacons. Stevens's job was to take oblique photographs whereby the contour of the terrain could be determined. In vertical photos the "relief" of the ground is reduced, particularly in high-altitude work. But oblique pictures can be taken of the same spot from two separated points in the air and, when compared, show the relative heights and conformations of the territory. The particular problem was the mapping of forty-nine square miles around Mount Washington in New Hampshire. A new apparatus imported from the famous Zeiss Laboratories in Germany, the Hugershoff pantograph, was used in plotting contours from the oblique photos.

Lacking darkroom facilities, Stevens set his staff of airplane mechanics to work building the huge troughs for developing the long rolls of forty or fifty feet of film in the girls' lavatory of a public-school building where there was a concrete floor and runoff from shower baths. Steve was working with them, mixing developer, setting up drying racks, and wading about in hip boots. Starting early in the morning he flew all day with Lieutenant Wade, taking pictures, then worked most of the night on the films. And flying was dangerous, particularly in the wartime planes then in use. They were flying all day *over* mountains when aviators used to fly miles to avoid one. But Lieutenant Wade—later one of the famous Round-the-World fliers —was not daunted, and mountains were no obstacle to a man like Stevens, who would bail out in a parachute at 24,000 feet as a summer-day pastime, a stunt Stevens did in June 1922, nearly landing in the Ohio River as a result.

After a hard day's flying and a night spent wading around in the improvised dark room, Stevens would often fall asleep in his chair, fully dressed. A short time later, at 5:30 A.M., Wade would breeze in and say: "A bright morning, Cap, let's go." And Stevens would shake himself, nod "Okay," and start all over again. This went on for days at a time. Though the job of contour mapping forty-nine square miles of mountain country took six weeks it would have taken two years with transit and level from the ground!

Aerial photography has progressed considerably since those days of the White Mountain Expedition in the early 1920's. A stereoscopic principle later came to be used in contour mapping, similar to the stereo photos taken with a double-lens camera in which the lenses are placed the approximate distance apart of the human eyes or wider. The pictures are viewed through the magnifying glasses of a stereoscope to produce relief. In aerial photography the difference in angle of only a few inches would be negligible in producing a "relief" image, so two photos are taken from the air from different points. These are printed on glass plate transparencies and viewed through a stereoscope arrangement which brings out all the relief, making contour mapping comparatively simple, and entirely accurate.

Between 1935 and 1937 more commercial air-photo work was done than in the previous ten years, but Stevens, promoted from Captain to Major, rested no more than he used to in the early days at McCook. On hot summer days, when most of the personnel would take a swim and rest, Steve could be seen in running trunks, trotting about the field. It was not primarily because he was interested in athletics. He felt that his job required him to be in condition, so he always kept himself in top-notch physical shape. The job, always, came first. On one occasion he was carrying one of his cameras and slipped. Rather than allow his precious instrument to be injured Steve held on to it, taking the brunt of the crash himself and breaking an arm, but the camera was saved!

Major Stevens exemplified the man completely happy in

his work. Possessing independent means he cared nothing for money, and therefore turned aside all efforts of commercial industry to lure him from the Army. A bachelor of simple tastes, he continued to be content with Army life and the pleasure embodied in his work—in his cameras and equipment, in the ever changing scene and new adventures he met.

The feats already mentioned are only a small part of Major Stevens's activities. He made an aerial photograph of the city of Sacramento in 1930, developed it in the plane, and dropped it within twelve minutes to a waiting newspaper representative. The picture appeared on the streets in the paper within an hour. He blazed the way for military photography which permits pictures to be taken day or night at altitudes that make a plane soundless and invisible. On leave from the Army, he went with an expedition exploring the hitherto unknown headwaters of the Amazon River, and several years later went to assist the National Geographic Society in exploration work in South America.

In collaboration with the National Geographic Society again, in the summer of 1934, Stevens made the historic stratosphere flight with Major Kepner and Captain Anderson, during which their balloon developed a rip in the underside and finally catapulted to the earth while millions of radio listeners heard the fliers' voices over a national radio hookup.

High above the Black Hills of South Dakota the balloon rose, until Major Kepner, speaking over the microphone, announced that they were 57,000 feet above the ground—

and that the underside of the balloon was ripped! ". . . We are going to have to come down," he said. "The bottom of the bag is ripped in several places underneath the catenary, and the balloon is rather difficult to manage. I don't know what to expect." Meanwhile, Stevens was clicking off his pictures and tending his instruments.

At 6:15 P.M., after some seven hours in the air, Kepner announced that they had descended to an altitude which permitted opening the gondola, impossible before this because of the thin air. And at 6:30 Stevens, speaking over the radio to General Westover in Washington, said: "We are about ready to jump. . . . We are down to around 13,000 feet and we are settling. . . . The bag is pretty well torn up. . . . There has been, in the bottom, a good deal of surging of air and descent is very rapid. I don't know . . . I am going to . . ."

That was the last listeners heard, until reports came in that the three fliers had jumped in parachutes. By that time the balloon was rushing to earth in a free fall, a fall so rapid that though the first man bailed out at 5000 feet the sphere was only 500 feet above ground when Kepner, last to jump, left it!

But all three survived the landing in a cornfield, and the following year Stevens and Anderson made the flight again with complete success, reaching an altitude of 72,395 feet. No—there has been no dearth of thrills in Major Stevens's career with his cameras.

He continued to keep busy at Wright Field. No job was too arduous or dirty for him to don greasy overalls and lend a hand. Almost any summer day as twilight approached, the lanky, sunbrowned figure with the friendly crinkles about the eyes could be seen trotting across the field for his constitutional. At the end of his run, when nearly everyone had left for home, he would make his way across the field to a clump of shrubbery nearly a mile from the hangars and throw himself on the ground in a bed of long grass. There he would lie on his back, gazing skyward until the first stars appeared, as though he dreamed of some day reaching them. Perhaps he was thinking of his pet dream— conquering by air lofty Mount Everest with its perpetual gales and storms. The man who had soared familiarly about the highest peaks of the Rockies and the Sierras as well as down into the Grand Canyon would speculate on what he would need to fly close to the summit of Everest, circle about the famous unscaled peak, and be lowered by rope ladder to the top of the world where he could take his pictures and be off again. Such an attempt seemed madness, but if the opportunity ever presented itself . . . Steve would do it!

Chapter 7

LIFESAVERS OF THE AIR

Edward L. Hoffman

High over the field the drone of an airplane sounds, the ship itself shrunken by distance into a tiny miniature which anxious eyes follow intently. A test pilot is putting a plane through rigorous maneuvers. Suddenly the wings begin to flutter. There is a mighty wrench as one of them folds, and an uncontrollable plane plunges earthward. Horrified, the men on the ground watch the plummeting plane. A gasp emerges from parted lips as a dark speck detaches itself from the plane and grows larger. "Pull the cord! Pull it, man!" they cry in their excitement. Then, as though the speck could hear them, a tiny white flutter of silk streams out from it. A billowing mass follows, blossoms magically into a giant umbrella, and the jumper is lowered gently to the ground.

Before 1925 such a lucky ending to disaster would have been too much to expect, for until that time the parachute was not reliably perfected. Although man first took to the air in 1783 (in a balloon), it was not until 142 years later that he possessed any safe means of emergency descent. The greatness of this achievement was attested on February 7, 1926, when President Coolidge, at the White House, awarded the Collier Trophy to Major Edward L. Hoffman for perfecting the parachute, the value of which had been thoroughly demonstrated by actual use the preceding year.

It was shortly after the Armistice that long, lanky, kindly eyed Ed Hoffman from Taylor Field, Montgomery, Alabama, was assigned to McCook Field, Dayton, Ohio, as Chief of the Equipment Section of the Engineering Division. Born in New York in 1884 and a student at the University of Utah and at Washington University in St. Louis, he enlisted in 1909 in the 24th United States Infantry as a private. At the end of two years' service he was commissioned Second Lieutenant. During nine years' service in the infantry, Hoffman was twice raised in rank, to First Lieutenant and Captain. No West Point type officer, he remained entirely uninterested in the purely military and had no ambition to shine as a smartly accoutered officer. Soon after receiving his commission as First Lieutenant, while in Mexico, he decided to enter aviation. Characteristically, he dismisses the decision casually by saying, "I just got tired walking around in the hot sun and dust of Mexico and decided to apply for transfer to the Air Service."

But his application and work in aeronautics were far from casual as he built up the background that was to prove so valuable in his development of the Life Preservers of the Air. An officer in the Aviation Section of the Signal Corps, he was trained in flying at Rockwell Field, North Island, and San Diego. At Kelly Field, Texas, he commanded various flying cadet aero squadrons in preparation for flying in France during the First World War. Later he served at Park Field, Millington, Tennessee, and at Taylor Field, Montgomery, Alabama, where he remained as commandant until his transfer to McCook Field—later known as Wright Field—in January 1919. As Material Section Chief at McCook, his duties included the testing and development of paints, fabrics, metals, and the like. His focus of interest, however, was upon parachutes, and it was at McCook that he was destined to carry on all his pioneering work.

Wandering about the hangars shortly after his arrival he found the sum total of the research that had been previously carried on: two parachutes, minus the harness, packed away in a small steel chest and tucked in a corner with the few tools that had been used in making them. Inquiry disclosed that two men in his section had been diligent enough in their attempts with the 'chutes, and had done some testing by dropping them from a De Havilland plane with fifty-pound weights attached. But there was little attention given to parachutes, for there were no funds with which to work and no encouragement.

The very futility of the situation seemed to fire Hoffman with determination. At the first meeting of section chiefs which he attended, he handed Colonel Bane a list of all the things on which he wanted to carry out research. "You're crazy!" Bane snapped, and the others agreed. But Hoffman refused to let the matter rest there. Later he retrieved his requisition from the wastepaper basket and at the next meeting put his proposal back on Bane's desk. Again it landed in the basket. But Hoffman was working C. F. Kettering's old trick. He had only one answer, "If I can beat the janitor to the wastebasket enough times, I'll wear 'em out!"

Persevere he did, in spite of four or five refusals, until finally, perhaps in sheer desperation, Bane said, in effect: "All right—hire a couple of guys, get a bolt of silk, and fool around with it if you must!" That was all Hoffman needed. After getting enough funds appropriated to procure silk, sewing machines, tools, and other material he immediately formed the nucleus of a parachute branch at McCook Field, employing special airplanes for testing, weights, dummies, and other necessary paraphernalia. Then he set to work in earnest, with the same dogged determination that had won him this chance, to make a parachute that would give a flier a chance for his life when his ship broke up in the air or caught fire.

Research, experiment, and test began practically "from scratch." While there were existing parachutes at the time, they were neither perfected nor standard Army equipment. So Major Hoffman's first step was to purchase samples of all the then existing parachutes, both foreign and domestic, including three parachutes without harness that had been sold to the government by a struggling American manufacturer. Exhaustive tests were carried on with all these types. Hoffman realized that the 'chutes must stand up under maximum strains and loads. He abandoned the in-conclusive testing with fifty-pound weights, and "Dummy Joe," the hero of a thousand jumps, came to life. Joe was a life-size figure, weighing 170 pounds, that simulated a live load in all the test jumps.

Heretofore little attention had been paid to size, shape, or any of the many factors except strength. Hoffman be-gan his experiments on various sizes of the "body"—or umbrella-like sustaining part of the parachute proper. He tested the length of the shroud lines. He experimented with the vents that control the escapement of the air. He experi-mented with the harness, the pack, methods of wearing—that is, seat or back packs—and with ways of controlling the oscillation, or swing, in the air as Dummy Joe de-scended.

By calculation it was determined that the terminal veloc-ity of a man falling free through the air would be approxi-mately at the rate of 350 miles per hour. Hoffman's goal, then, was to design a parachute that could safely open and sustain a weight of 200 pounds traveling at that velocity. Another obstacle arose here: Dummy Joe, for all his will-ingness to be subjected to innumerable drops, could not pull the rip cord after a free fall of sixteen seconds. So Major Hoffman took the time fuze from the nose of an artillery shell and devised a mechanism that would allow a sixteen-second fall before pulling the cord.

Assisting Major Hoffman were Guy Ball and Floyd Smith, who had been making parachute jumps for years in county fairs where a balloon ascension and jump were regular features. Their practical experience was of great value to Hoffman's research.

Weeks went into months as the routine of calculation, experiment, and test drops went on. Hoffman, who had never paid particular attention to military furbelows, could be found around McCook Field at all hours, wearing almost anything but a uniform. Often he wore a civilian shirt, open at the throat, and golf knickers, much to the disdain of more orthodox officers. It was the summer of 1920, after about six months' work, that he was raised to the rank of Major, which to Hoffman merely meant the privilege of oak leaves on his shoulders for parades or other rare occasions that found him in full uniform. And almost invariably, after a parade or review that required full uniform, he would sneak into the hangars and say: "Let's get this stuff off and get into working clothes, boys," which usually meant mechanic's overalls.

Two tyes of parachutes had been under experiment: the free type in which the 'chute was carried by the pilot independently of the plane, and the static type in which the 'chute was attached to the body of the plane and was released by the jump of the pilot. Hoffman soon decided the free-type parachute was more versatile and practical. It allowed the pilot greater freedom of movement in the plane and permitted delayed drops, which was a safety factor that eliminated to a great extent the possibility of the 'chute fouling on part of the tail surfaces of the airplane.

The greatest load on a parachute occurs at the moment it opens and the free fall is suddenly checked. The time-fuze mechanism proved too cumbersome, and further calculation showed that a load of 400 pounds released from a plane flying at 120 miles per hour would put as much strain on the 'chute, if not more, as a delayed drop of sixteen seconds. It became possible to simplify the test drops and still acquire the same strength data.

In some of the tests certain of the rigging lines broke during the drop. Hoffman became convinced that a means must be found to record the strain on each individual cord. He devised a mechanical arrangement that measured and recorded the shock each cord received. A great deal of attention was also given to vents, ring vents, puckered vents, and Major Hoffman's own development, first used by him, multiple vents.

A policy of encouraging private enterprise was followed. Industry was kept informed of all developments as they occurred at McCook Field and given problems to solve. Since no private manufacturers, at the time, had the facilities for test drops, their work consisted mainly in making parachutes to order from the sketches submitted to them.

Each problem that arose was met and eventually conquered. One detail was the necessity of finding a silk sufficiently fine-woven for parachute purposes. Hoffman determined that a silk known as "22 mummie"—the grading term used—was necessary. Unfortunately this silk was not produced anywhere in the world. Hoffman worked through a silk broker who in turn went to the Mitsui Company, the largest importing and industrial trading company in Japan. A single silk mill was found in Japan that would install the expensive and unorthodox machinery necessary to manufacture 22-mummie silk. This gave Hoffman the material he needed with maximum strength and minimum weight. It was compact when packed, yet still porous enough to let air pass through and prevent excessive pendulum swing otherwise caused by air "spilling" from one side or the other of the 'chute.

When finally a parachute body could be accurately designed to meet strength tests, Major Hoffman turned his attention to pack, harness, lanyard, and other parts of the equipment.

He was engaged in constant activity, not only in directing and supervising the work but in taking part. He went up in the test planes and hunched over a work bench with his assistants. He filed a safety-belt clasp with the practiced hand and eye of the born mechanic, made drawings, fashioned parts, and worked with subordinate officers on the field or in the laboratory as a matter of course.

Two years passed before it was felt that a parachute could be built to which a man might safely entrust his life. Knowledge of his work generated an insistent demand that forced Major Hoffman to issue an order for the construction of 550 parachutes, although he would have preferred more time for testing and experiment. So it was that, under pressure, he designed the parachute known as Type A.

Dummy Joe, by this time, was making regular jumps safely. It was decided that the time was ripe for the first live jump. Colonel Bane tells about it this way:

"I remember, very distinctly, that this particular test was

a great strain on everybody. It was like sitting on a hot stove, to watch the ship maneuvering into place over the field and seeing Floyd Smith finally leap overboard—and the great relief of everybody when the parachute 'worked.' After this it became a question as to the next steps. I thought that everybody should jump, and privately made up my mind to sneak out some day and make a jump at Wilbur Wright Field on the other side of Dayton, for the purpose of encouraging others. I think I probably delayed doing this while getting my courage up. At any rate, I delayed too long, for one day Hoffman walked into my office with the parachute folded up under his arm and the harness still on and told me with great glee that he had just made the first jump ever made by a commissioned officer of the Air Corps. This, of course, ruined all of my plans and truthfully, I must say, was rather a relief, as I made up my mind then that I would only jump if I had to leave an airplane because of mechanical failure or fire."

So, before he would approve the order for 'chutes to be used by the Air Corps, Major Hoffman himself jumped in one. The 550 parachutes were made and delivered and they were in use for some time, giving perfect satisfaction. The first life preserver of the air had proved itself. Members of the Air Corps learned to use it, making over a thousand separate jumps.

Besides making the drawings and giving specifications for the manufacture of these parachutes, Major Hoffman also designed the vent operating mechanism, reinforcing cordage, and Dee rings. Many other problems remained for solution, a tragedy bringing home one of them. Strength testing had been one of the primary considerations in the parachute research; it had been tacitly assumed that a parachute would open in the air. During a practice jump Sergeant Washburn fell to his death, due to the failure of his parachute to open. It took nearly a year of intensive study to solve this problem. Major Hoffman made slow-motion movies of the opening of the chute, among other observations, and it was found that the fault was inherent in the design of the parachute's mouth. After correcting the design to insure positive opening, Hoffman reasoned that tests should not only simulate average conditions but aggravate them, that parachutes should open safely under the worst possible service conditions. This resulted in the requirement that 'chutes must open with *three twists* in the shroud lines, a condition more extreme than any average usage might likely present.

Still Major Hoffman felt he had not removed all danger. He continued his experiments and conceived the idea that a parachute could be designed which would inflate even if the mouth were held shut. He gave one of his men the basic idea, and the development was carried out in the Post swimming pool. The pool was used as a "towing basin," and the parachutes were inflated under water. The principle was so successful that its application was patented by the man who worked it out. Months after the usefulness of the parachute of his design had been demonstrated, Major Hoffman found that the spirit of daring and indifference to danger was so great among the fliers at McCook Field that it was hard to convince them that they ought to wear the new lifesaving device. Again and again the Major would be chagrined to find that a pilot was ready to leave the ground without his life preserver. Pilots offered excuses that the pack was uncomfortable or that it interferred with manipulation of controls.

The day came when Lieutenant Harold R. Harris, Chief Test Pilot of the Flying Section at McCook, wearing the new back-pack parachute, took up a plane for a test flight. Harris had been trained in Europe and America and was one of the most valuable test pilots in the Army. In the air the wings of Harris's plane began to flutter. With a sudden crack one of them broke away, leaving Harris with a semi-wingless ship out of control. He jumped—and the parachute worked perfectly, landing him in a grape arbor, unhurt except for a few scratches. It was a mishap that otherwise would have meant almost certain death.

This dramatized the practical value of parachutes to the other fliers, and the difficulties of making pilots wear them grew less. Shortly after Harris's jump, Major General Patrick, then Chief of Air Corps, issued orders making parachutes standard equipment of the Corps and prohibiting flights without them. Harris, whose life had been saved by the 'chute, continued to assist the development of aviation. Later he became Chief of the Flying Section and still later in commercial aviation became an operations executive of Pan American Airways.

That first forced jump of Lieutenant Harris was responsible, too, for the spontaneous origin of the picturesque

"Caterpillar Club," an organization with no by-laws, no constitution, no dues, and only one requirement for membership. To belong, a flier had to save his life by bailing out of a disabled plane and taking to his parachute. How the club received its name and just when it started has been the subject of argument, but there seems little doubt that Harris was the original charter member, and that the name refers to the silken cords and fabric of the parachute, product of the silkworm, which is in reality a caterpillar. A Caterpillar Club *Journal* kept by Air Corps officials tells many a thrilling tale of fliers now alive who, but for the 'chute, would have cracked up with their planes and been killed or seriously injured. Lindbergh was the fifteenth man to join the club and was the first fourth-degree member, with four forced jumps to safety.

General Patrick's order marked the end of the pioneering development of the parachute, but not the end of Major Hoffman's labors. He set to work to develop a wind tunnel where truly scientific methods could be applied in the testing and development of new models of parachutes. All shapes, types, and sizes of parachutes underwent rigorous analysis, with experiments along radically new lines. Heretofore only the circular parachute had been considered. Hoffman's experiments revealed that a triangular shape allowed slower descent and was more efficient because it would sustain more weight. He evolved, also, a funnel-like construction on the rear corner of the triangle which allowed air to escape in a jet, propelling the parachute forward, allowing greater steerability and reducing oscillation. Following his established procedure of testing for maximum safety, Hoffman required the 'chutes to open with as many as *eight* full twists in the shroud lines.

Still he refused to rest on his laurels. "What about transport plane passengers?" he said. "In the event of accident why not give them a chance for their white alley? In the Army we get paid to risk our necks. But in commercial transport the public pays for the privilege of dying!" It had been a dream of his for a long time to design a plane-carrying parachute which would lower the entire aircraft and passengers safely to the ground in the event of accident. Shortly after receiving the Collier Trophy for his invaluable work Major Hoffman was assigned to the Department of Commerce to give him an opportunity to work on his pet idea. It resulted in the world's largest parachute. On November 18, 1930, a primary training plane, weighing 2500 pounds and carrying Major Hoffman as operator and Captain Street as pilot, was equipped with a triangular parachute. This 'chute, eighty feet in diameter, was tested at Fairfield at an altitude of 5000 feet. When the signal was given the 'chute was released; the huge, billowing cloud of tough, fine silk snapped into shape and safely lowered the plane to the ground with hardly a perceptible shock as it landed. The descent was steady and on an even keel. No oscillation, no rotation, and a descent at the rate of only twelve feet per second were items in the amazing performance of this new device. And once again Major Hoffman himself was among the first to stake his own safety on his brain-child. The entire device weighed only 125 pounds and was stowed in the center section of the ship.

Not all his later work was done at McCook. In February 1925, he was transferred to Cincinnati for duty with the Air Corps Reserve unit stationed at Grisard Field. Later he selected and established Lunken Airport in Cincinnati, and after three years' absence returned to McCook, by that time known as Wright Field.

Other improvements and modifications were developed by Major Hoffman. They included a quick-attachable pack for emergencies, new harness, all-metal safety belt for pilots, gunner's belt, parachutes for dropping and igniting flares, and targets of new design. In all his work he left no foreseeable detail to chance before experimenting. Not a strut, brace, bolt, or lanyard went into his experimental models that he did not personally work on or inspect. His willingness to risk his own life and the lives of others on the 'chutes he built rested not on any spirit of bravado and derring-do, but upon thorough, careful workmanship and full faith and knowledge in the reliability of his tested designs.

Chapter 8

AVIATION AND THE AUTO INDUSTRY

William B. Stout

In August 1925, the infant American aviation industry was electrified to hear that Henry Ford had entered the field of aviation and purchased the Stout Metal Airplane Company. The news was a shot in the arm to the slump which aviation had suffered since the end of World War I. Excited and optimistic comment rippled outward in financial and industrial circles. If Henry Ford, that canny self-made man whose Model-T flivver had overrun the roads, that unorthodox motor-maker who had become America's leading industrialist—if he was going to bring his mass-production methods to the building of commercial airplanes, American commercial aviation would finally amount to something. And if Congress would just get around to passing an Air Commerce Act (it did in 1926), American commercial flying might catch up with European airlines.

Progress there soon was. The moral backing which resulted from the mere association of the Ford Company with aviation provided impetus for expansion at a critical period in the history of the industry. Said an anonymous commentator in a Detroit paper at the time Ford took over the Stout Company, "Ford's entrance into aviation means progress in three departments: commercial flying, passenger flying, and national defense. . . . If Stout never did anything else for aviation but interest the Fords, he did a great service for our civilization."

The man who "sold" aviation to Ford was, like the other men in this book, a man of many firsts. He developed the first American all-metal airplane. He designed the first split-type landing gear used on commercial planes. One-time president of the Society of Automotive Engineers and Chief Engineer of the Aircraft Division of the Packard Motor Car Company, he served as Technical Adviser to the American Aircraft Board during the First World War. His name? William Bushnell Stout.

The story of Bill Stout is the chronicle of a radical in industry. It is the semi-tragedy of a man years ahead of his time. His revolutionary spirit took form, not in politics or social activity, but in creative engineering genius. When the Army, for example, was concerned only with biplanes Bill Stout designed an unusual "bat-wing" plane, an internally braced monoplane covered with plywood, which was immediately dubbed "The Cootie" for its obvious resemblance to the pest of World War I. Nothing came of the Cootie then. But twenty years later many features of that same basic design were to be found in the experimental "flying wings." So it has always been with Stout. And by the time the world catches up to his ideas he has passed on ahead, impatient of the delay.

The origin of this scholarly-looking, lean-faced man's interest in things aeronautical goes back more than a decade before the turn of the century. Beside a small lake in Illinois the Reverend James F. Stout stood with his small son, Bill, watching the graceful maneuvers of gulls as they swept down the wind in long swoops, their white wings gleaming against the blue of the sky. Circling, dipping, soaring, never still yet always behaving with effortless energy and perfect grace, they held the boy's absorbed attention.

"What kind of birds are those, Daddy?" the four-year-old inquired. "What makes them do all those tricks—how can they do them?"

Other heads had pondered that question without arriving at a workable answer. From before Leonardo da Vinci's time until the Wrights flew it was to remain a question largely unanswered. But the Reverend Stout explained as best he could, and the boy followed with breathless interest all his father had to say. "Even now," the minister concluded, "men are trying to learn the secrets of the birds so that some day they may fly through the air the way those gulls fly. Perhaps you, my son, can be the one to show them how to do it."

Those words were not without prophetic meaning. Since then William Bushnell Stout, though not the first to fly, has blazed a trail through the clouds many times for other men to follow.

Stimulated by his father's words and his natural inclinations, young Stout came to set mastery of the air as his goal. Throughout his early childhood Bill bent every effort to learn what he could of the early experiments in flying. Poor, meager scraps they were, for half a century ago aeronautical knowledge was small and aeronautical experiment undignified by the title of "science." "Art" was the word commonly used—"the art of flying." And flying was a foolhardy game over which gray heads waggled disapprovingly. A crackpot idea!

Nevertheless, as Bill grew up, he continually sought and absorbed every shred of information on his obsession—flying. In 1894 the *Youth's Companion* magazine ran a series of articles with pictures and descriptions of how to make airplane models from cardboard and rubber bands. Bill followed them carefully and built his first airplane. Then came the moment of anxiety and suspense. Would it fly?

This first practical experiment was a great deal more significant to Bill Stout than a similar attempt made by a young lad would be today. There were none of the present-day "assembly kits," or knock-down models so designed that a boy need merely put them together to make them fly. Indeed, nine years were to pass before the Wrights' historical first flight would be made at Kitty Hawk. With bated breath young Stout took his model outdoors, wound his rubber-band motor, started it—and it flew! It was only a short flight, a few, a very few, feet. But it flew. For a magical second or two, it had lifted free of the earth and had imitated the flight of the gulls that ten years before had fascinated the boy.

The first airplane was more than a workable toy to young Bill. It was more than a successful experiment. This fragile model might be composed only of cardboard and rubber bands but what these flimsy, simple materials had been made to accomplish might surely be repeated with better materials to better effect. With wood, canvas, and metal in place of cardboard, with engines instead of rubber bands, what greater flights might not be made? New impetus was given to Stout's ambition. Fixed anew in his thoughts was his determination to fly, himself, as his tiny model had flown. From the boyish thrill that came at seeing his model plane fly he would progress to the extreme exaltation of being carried in a plane. To make it swoop and dip like a gull in accordance with his own desires and finally to land it safely just where he wanted, this became the one thing in life worth striving for.

It was in Mankato, Minnesota, about a hundred miles south of the Twin Cities of Minneapolis and St. Paul, that Stout had this first-hand experience at flying. The Reverend Stout had previously moved his family from Quincy, following the call of his church. In the next four years, while going to high school, Bill continued his quest for knowledge of planes and flying. By the time he was eighteen, when most boys are thinking of the unaccustomed freedom and privileges of adult life, Bill was writing and illustrating articles about airplanes. He reasoned that what was of such paramount interest to himself must be equally interesting to other boys, and the information which he had so laboriously dug out and accumulated he passed along to others. Perhaps others who might be as interested but lacked his dogged perseverance could nevertheless profit by his research.

It was a period of flux and change. Old ideas were gradually giving way to new facts. Though flying was still far from an actuality and was regarded by many as a foolhardy dream rather than a real possibility, there were those who admitted the possibility that there might be something to this crazy business. Although no definitely successful flight had been made, the attempts of some of those early pioneers were gradually coming closer to the goal and were arousing interest and world comment. So it is not surprising that these first articles of Stout's immediately commanded great interest from his audience of boys, who through all the ages have thrown their youthful enthusiasm into new fields.

In 1899 Bill Stout went to Hamline University, leaving in his second year to go to the University of Minnesota where there were greater opportunities for technical education. His goal, a degree in mechanical engineering, was almost achieved when, in the spring of 1903, tragedy struck him. His too avid search for knowledge and his too eager pursuit of it defeated their own ends; his eyesight failed him. After many consultations with doctors he received an ultimatum: for two years at least he would be unable to use his eyes for any reading. Indeed, it was extremely doubtful whether he would ever again be able to read more than a newspaper headline. This dreadful setback forced him to leave college a month before the end of the term and deprived him of both his degree and credits for his work for that term.

Since Bill could not use his eyes for studying, he started out a month later for Europe. He had always wanted to go abroad. This was his chance. All that was lacking was money but this obstacle, which might have stopped many, Bill took in his stride.

One way or another he got to New York, then worked his way to London. On the ship was a young chap from the University of Kansas named McRae, also working his way. They decided to team up and together the two boys traveled over Europe all summer, doing anything and everything which might earn money to take them on to the next town. When all else failed they would go out on a street corner in the evening. McRae would play a guitar or a mandolin while Stout would draw pictures on a blackboard and give chalk talks.

Another source of small income was a series of articles Stout wrote, despite his doctor's injunctions, which were published in the Minneapolis *Times*.

In this vagabond fashion, they went through England, Scotland, France, Belgium, Holland, Germany, Switzerland, and Italy. Finally, late in that year, Stout wound up in London, a penniless, lonesome, homesick boy. Desperately anxious to return home, after a week of fruitless effort he finally wangled a job on a cattle boat America-bound.

He was quartered in the hold and did a regular seaman's work. Although he was almost starving he could not bring himself to eat the miserable food served to the crew. For three days he fasted, each day worse than the last. Then his resourcefulness came to his aid. He sought out the cook and volunteered to peel a bushel of potatoes for him. From that day until the boat put into New York Harbor he had plenty of decent food to eat.

After Stout's return home his eye trouble still prevented his reading, but by using a typewriter he managed to continue his writing and sold many short features and articles to various magazines and newspapers. Still his eyes were not improving. Time after time his doctors reported that there was little hope. But Bill needed his eyes, and he was not discouraged. "These doctors don't know everything," he would say. "I'll fool them yet."

Perhaps time was all that was needed, or perhaps his sheer persistence and refusal to admit defeat turned the tide. At any rate, after two years his eyes finally did begin to improve. This enabled him to take a regular position on the St. Paul *Dispatch* where he started a boys' department in the paper, under the name of "Jack Kneiff." At the same time he taught manual training and mechanical arts in the Mechanical Arts High School in St. Paul. "Jack Kneiff" almost immediately became one of the most popular features in the paper and after a while was successfully syndicated. At the same time he started "Boy Island" under the auspices of the *Dispatch* at Bald Eagle Lake, about twenty miles from St. Paul. Here was a government of, by, and for boys. Once the project was well under way, Stout acted purely in a supervisory capacity. The boys did everything.

They had their own municipal government, elected their own mayor and city councilors, and had their own street and police departments. Few cities were run in a more efficient and orderly manner.

All this time, however, Bill Stout's interest in his first love, aviation, had not waned. In 1907, he delivered an address on aviation before the Engineers' Society of Minneapolis and displayed airplane models loaned by Chanute. He presented lantern slides showing other models by Chanute and the Wrights, as well as planes in actual flight. From then on, the series of events that were eventually to move Stout into his niche in aviation followed with increasing rapidity. He made a six-thousand-mile motorcycle tour of Europe and built a radically new type of motorcycle on his return. This, in turn, resulted eventually in his being made Chief Engineer for the Schurmeir Motor Truck Company. In 1912, he became automobile and aviation editor of the Chicago *Tribune*—his first real aviation job—and was a regular contributor to *Motor Age*. Shortly afterward he founded *Aviation Age*, first aviation magazine ever published in America.

Two years later he accepted a job as Chief Engineer with the Scripps-Booth Automobile Company, whose new car he designed. He had become General Sales Manager of the Packard Motor Car Company when, in 1916, they started an aviation division and asked Stout to become its first Chief Engineer. The war broke out a year later and the Packard engineers, headed by Stout, went to Washington to help the government design and build the Liberty engine. Stout did not take a commission, realizing that his experience and knowledge made him more valuable as a civilian at home, and he was appointed Technical Adviser to the Aircraft Board.

This was a very real, very necessary job, particularly in view of the comparative dearth of men with background or knowledge of aeronautical engineering in America. In a spacious office commanding a view of McCook Field from the Air Building at Dayton, Ohio, sat Bill Stout, looking more like a teacher of manual arts in a boys' school. Hollow-cheeked, with tousled hair, necktie askew, and clothes apparently a matter of indifference, Stout sat behind a desk piled high with technical data, completely surrounded by diagrams and charts of the multitudinous engines and planes being produced and offered for production to the Army Air Service. He was surrounded, too, by the best brains of the automotive industry upon which the infant American aviation industry had drawn. Colonels Vincent, Marmon, and C. F. Kettering were a few. Ralph De Palma, famous automobile driver, was in the test-pilot section as was "Caley" Bragg, millionaire sportsman and former speedboat racer.

One of Stout's first big jobs was "licking the bugs"—eliminating technical difficulties—in the design of the then new Liberty engine, in order to make it practical for production. Stout's efforts were not confined to the office or factory. He was on the flying field, up in the air, in the hangars, talking to pilots and mechanics and anyone else who could and would answer his questions. Always he was on the trail of practical operating experience which would bring academic theory down to earth and enable him to make better airplanes. The eventual great success of the Liberty engine, which as one of its greatest exploits carried the American Round-the-World fliers, and which was perhaps the leading water-cooled engine of its time, is no small tribute to Stout's ability.

Shortly after the war, in the spring of 1919, the Bureau of Military Aeronautics, of which Colonel Thurman Bane was Chief in Washington, and the Bureau of Aircraft Production were consolidated at McCook Field as a unified technical and development center, under the command of Colonel Bane. Only a sprinkling of officers was carried over from wartime days. Jimmy Johnson, Al Johnson, Frank Hambly, and J. D. Hill were a few of the pioneer civilian instructors and test pilots who still carried on.

During the war, and at postwar McCook, design concentrated almost exclusively upon the biplane. But Stout, always scornful of the accepted and orthodox when improvements might be made, designed a high-wing monoplane from which all struts, wires, and other wind obstructions had been eliminated. It was completely revolutionary in design and appearance, looking so much like the trench pests of the war that it was immediately dubbed "Stout's Cootie." Jimmie Johnson was assigned to fly the weird-looking plane, and made several fairly successful flights in it. But in the opinion of the officers at McCook the ship did not hold much promise as a miltary craft and nothing further was done with it.

Its importance, overlooked perhaps by all but Stout, was

the fact that it undoubtedly marked a radical innovation in aircraft design. It was the first thick-wing, internally trussed monoplane constructed in the United States. So radical was it, in fact, that its theory and design were some fifteen to twenty years in advance of the aviation industry. But in 1919 it was just another freak idea, peculiarly shaped with its triangular single wing that extended back to the tail surface like a bat-wing. An interesting sidelight on this is the fact that within recent years almost the identical design has been again brought out in the "Flying Wing."

Although the early monoplane—the Cootie—was never to see service, Stout had learned a great deal more of aerodynamic principles and airplane building from it. This knowledge he put to advantage in 1920 when he left government service and organized his first aviation company. He wanted to build a remodeled bat-wing plane. It was during this period that Stout made his first, indirect contact with Henry Ford. Ford's chief engineer, William Mayo, had just spent the previous summer traveling in Europe to secure the latest information about aviation progress abroad, where already Imperial Airways was operating successfully between London and Paris, and other airlines were linking the capitals of Europe. In the fall, Mayo dropped in on Stout, looked over what he was doing, and offered some of the information he had gathered in Europe. From that time on Mayo would frequently stop in to see Stout, intimating not only that he was personally interested but that Henry Ford also was interested in the way in which new developments were being carried forward.

It was a characteristic of Stout's that he was always willing to back his ideas with his own money, but in the formation of his aviation company additional capital was needed. Stout approached a group of twenty-five Detroit businessmen whom he considered able to invest and, if necessary, to lose their investments. He appealed to them on the grounds not that they would make money by investing in his company, but that they owed it to their city, to the development of aviation, in short, to the nation, as public-spirited men, to put in a thousand dollars each. And he promised them only that they would very likely never see their money again.

Bill Stout's facility with words and his strictly unorthodox approach enabled him to "sell" his apparently altruistic proposition to a group of shrewd, hard-headed businessmen. He had the knack of making a comparatively commonplace happening sound like an absorbing adventure. He had the gift of boring incisively into an idea and bringing out a significant point with an apt meaning to his audience. He had the genius of dramatizing a dry technical matter into one of absorbing interest. And behind his talk were always a deep conviction of truth and a solid basis of knowledge and ability.

The Stout Engineering Company with its new funds conducted further experiments on the bat-wing plane and began to build a revolutionary, all-metal Air Sedan. In February 1923, newspapers in Detroit and across the country carried stories of the successful test flights of the Stout Air Sedan with Walter Lees at the controls. Again Stout had swerved widely from the orthodox and produced a plane far in advance of the field. The new, all-metal ship was of duralumin, strong as steel at one-third the weight. It was powered by only a ninety-horsepower OX motor, yet it carried three passengers in addition to the pilot and gas load. The same OX motor in wartime planes had been able to carry only one person in addition to the pilot. This was clear evidence of the merit of the new design.

The ship had been tested in the wind tunnel at M. I. T. It featured Stout's development of the thick, internally stressed, single wing, and was so constructed that the two halves of the wing could fold back for storing the ship in a space no larger than the average garage. The metal Air Sedan was built with the revolutionary split-type landing gear, instead of the customary all-wheels-on-one-axle construction which then prevailed. Another unusual feature was the completely detachable engine unit. Everything connected with the engine, except the outside gas line, could be detached from the plane by loosening four master bolts. This feature was based on the sound practical idea that service need not be interrupted for engine overhauls. Instead, the engine could be slipped out and another put in place in a short time.

Perhaps it was the attention paid to the practical features, and the idea, always in the near background of Stout's mind, that aviation would have to adapt itself to mass production and the commercial market that helped stimulate Ford's interest. After the Air Sedan, and later an Air Pullman, had been built, Mr. Mayo showed real interest in what Stout was doing. Henry Ford, he explained, was not personally interested in aviation, but he saw its possibilities and was interested in it primarily as a field for development for his son, Edsel. "Why don't you write Edsel Ford a letter," Mayo said, "and tell him just what he could do for aviation?"

Characteristically, Stout sat down the next day and wrote his letter, suggesting two things Ford could do for aviation in Detroit: first, that there should be a commercial field nearer than Selfridge, since for every test it was necessary to drag a plane thirty-six miles from the factory and back again, and second that a new engine should be designed and put on the market. The best engines then available were the OX-5 and the Hispano-Suiza. The Liberty motors, odd as it now sounds, were considered too big for commercial work.

There was no answer to Stout's letter for over four months. Ford's way of operating was one of quiet investigation and thorough probing before commitment. Then Mayo met Stout one day and said, in effect, "How would you like to have a landing field and factory for about a dollar a year?"

Stout said he would like it very much indeed, and the next day, accompanied by Mayo, he inspected the terrain around Dearborn, met Edsel Ford, and personally explained the whole proposition to him. The younger Ford was not wholly sold. "I'll write you five letters," Stout said, "that will convince you that you should invest in this."

Bill Stout writes good letters and these must have been

good, indeed, for Edsel Ford began to think aviation and to sell the idea to his father. Edsel bought a thousand dollars' worth of stock in Stout's company, as did Henry Ford and Mayo. Stout was asked to submit sketches for the kind of building he wanted. In sixty days the building was up and Stout had moved in and begun the building of half a dozen Liberty-engined passenger planes. This was in 1924. One day Henry Ford walked in and inspected the plant from end to end, showing great interest in the rapid progress that had been made.

"Well, Mr. Stout," he said, "I must tell you I'm very much surprised. I had no idea you had this factory equipped in any such thorough manner and were going ahead as you are." Less than a year later Ford made another visit to the plant and saw the ships almost completed. Mayo asked what Stout planned to do with the planes when they were ready. Bill explained that he was planning to run them on an express service between Detroit and Chicago. Mayo admitted that the Ford Company might be interested in them. Shortly afterward they were purchased by the Ford Company, and the Ford freight service to Chicago was started—the first American airline!

Henry Ford at this time was a frequent visitor, genuinely interested in the whole project. It was his custom to stop in, unannounced, and have a look around. On one of these casual inspection trips he said to Stout, "It seems to me that this thing has gotten to the point where somebody should put a lot of money behind it and carry it through the development period to a successful business. I don't see why the Ford Motor Company shouldn't do just that."

Ford made an offer of two-for-one, and Stout had to go to all his subscribers—over a hundred of them by now—with the news that they were to double the money they had expected never to see again. Since they had subscribed to the venture in the beginning because of their interest in flying rather than in making money, they were not anxious to withdraw. Mr. Ford agreed that if he took over production, the original group could go ahead with the operations. The group went into the project enthusiastically as partners of Ford, with twice as much money as they had had at the start. The airline was established as Stout Air Services between Detroit and Grand Rapids. Later this became the Detroit-Toledo-Chicago airline, which is still in operation, although now as a division of United Airlines. (When Stout sold out to United, all the investors' money was once more doubled, yielding a return of four thousand dollars for each thousand invested. This in a proposition in which the only guarantee had been that they would never see their money again!)

After Ford's purchase of Stout's factory, the designer set to work to produce the Ford all-metal transport ship, which Admiral Byrd was subsequently to use on his flight to the North Pole. Stout, having demonstrated the basic worth of his belief in a metal plane, was confronted with the necessity of turning out by production methods a plane of a type never before so produced in this country.

Following the basic design of the earlier Junker metal plane, the Ford trimotored plane which Stout built faced many problems. There was an explosion hazard. The hollow metal wings in earlier planes collected gasoline vapor. Sometimes, when the hot exhaust gases from the motors reached this vapor, a terrific explosion would follow and wreck the ship. This disadvantage in the foreign-made metal planes Stout remedied by placing ventilating holes in the leading edge of the wing. Another problem involved fabricating the tools for the manufacture of the metal-skinned monsters. On fabric wings it had been a comparatively simple matter to stretch the fabric over the framework. But riveting the duralumin-sheet skin over the metal ribs presented entirely new problems. Indeed, every step of metal fabrication offered new, never-before-solved problems. Stout evolved mandrils, some of them twelve feet long and ingeniously constructed to reach into the wing to do the riveting job. In a similar way each problem, as it arose, was met and licked, and the Ford trimotors finally rode the skies.

The rest is aviation history. Although the Ford Company is no longer active in aviation and the metal monoplane has become commonplace, Stout's achievement will never be forgotten: his persuasive tongue and skilled designer's pen gave fresh life to a stagnating industry. By enlisting the resources of the giant automotive industry he proved that commercial aviation was a practical possibility and an indispensable method of transportation for modern society.

Chapter 9

WATER WINGS

Edward O. McDonnell

This is the story of an aviation financier who had a reputation for making conservative, careful investments, who appeared to be a typical, indoor-type, desk executive—and who held the Congressional Medal of Honor for bravery.

Henry Ford's successful venture in building Bill Stout's all-metal trimotor planes and his establishment of an air-freight service gave the aviation industry a powerful boost out of the doldrums that set in after World War I. But this was not the only encouragement aviation received. In 1925 the generous Kelly Air Mail Act was passed, and in 1926 the Air Commerce Act went into effect, providing long-needed government regulation and encouragement to airlines. Then in 1927 Charles A. Lindbergh flew the Atlantic in a dramatic solo nonstop that touched off a burst of public enthusiasm in Europe and America as no previous flight had ever done. Suddenly aviation was in the public limelight. No longer was interest confined to obscure experiments, scattered barnstorming, and neglected military development. The man on the street in America became almost overnight air-conscious and air-crazy, while those with money to invest or speculate in the stock market in 1928 and 1929 clamored to purchase aviation securities. Anything to do with planes or flying was acclaimed by people eager to place their money in the magical new industry. And there was, naturally, no dearth of aviation companies offering many and varied stock issues. These the optimistic public subscribed to willingly and bought freely. Mergers and consolidations piled up paper values to tremendous heights that were out of all proportion to their actual worth. Little thought was given to the potential market for the products of these companies or to the vast technical developments still necessary before the American commercial aviation structure would be complete or even well founded.

There was chicanery and charlatanism, as well, on many sides. Too many aviation companies were devoted to stock-selling and too few to flying. They were operated by men whose ears were attuned more to the sound of a stock ticker than a radial motor. So, inevitably, when the crash of 1929 came, such unsound organizations remained only in the rueful memory of their investors.

Among the few investment firms that weathered the crash was one company which dealt conscientiously and successfully with the complex problem of investing the public's money in sound and worthwhile aviation securities. Seated at the president's desk of that company was a short, stocky man, mild and diffident of speech, with graying hair above a still youthful face, the guiding genius of the financial structure known as the National Aviation Company, Edward Orrick McDonnell.

At a time when anything to do with aviation stocks was booming and wild speculation and unbridled optimism ran high, Eddie McDonnell was conservative. During subsequent years he remained conservative in his business. Friends who had known him long and intimately all sadly agreed on the futility of trying to get a stock-market tip from Eddie. Not that he would bluntly refuse. But the quiet McDonnell voice, with still a hint of the Southern accent of his native Baltimore, would recommend some such ultraconservative investment stock as American Telephone and Telegraph, United States Steel, Standard Oil, or the like.

All this suggests a man whose life was bounded by the staid, prosaic conventionalities of the business office, a man whose greatest adventure might have been a hole-in-one at the country club. The record shows otherwise.

In the Medal of Honor list of the American Army and Navy there appears the name of Ensign Edward O. McDonnell, U. S. N.—

> For extraordinary heroism in battle, engagements of Vera Cruz April 21st. and 22nd., 1914: posted on the roof of the Terminal Hotel and landing, he established a signal station there and maintained communications between the troops and the ships. At this exposed post he was continually under fire. One man was killed and

three wounded at his side during two days' fighting. He showed extraordinary heroism and striking courage and maintained his station in the highest degree of efficiency. All signals got through, largely due to his heroic devotion to duty.

This direct quote of the Navy's usually unemotional citation accompanies our country's highest military honor, awarded to Eddie McDonnell—the Congressional Medal of Honor.

No, Eddie McDonnell in the Navy days was hardly a careful conservative. As a naval flier in the First World War, McDonnell, assigned to an Italian squadron on the Austro-Italian front, made what is believed the first flight by an American officer over the Italian lines. He was in the crew of a bomber that made a single-handed raid on an Austro-German airdome—an exploit that earned him a Silver Medal for valor. He manned the guns in a two-seater bomber raiding U-boat bases at Bruges. On another occasion he piloted the then new Caproni bomber over the historic Alps. So Eddie McDonnell was no "desk-flier." And it is due in no small measure to his experience as airplane pioneer flier, designer, and pilot that his knowledge of the aviation industry, from the hangars up, made him valuable behind the president's desk of an investment company.

Eddie McDonnell was born under what superstitious folk might consider a handicap, making his appearance in this world on Friday, November 13, 1891, in Baltimore, Maryland. Certainly, judging by his Navy exploits, Mc-

Donnell never placed any importance on the jinx numerals of his birth date. He attended school at Baltimore Polytechnic, and from early youth his determination crystallized into the desire for a Navy career. Ever-present, too, was his zest for action and adventure that led in later years to big-game hunting in remote parts of the globe.

His desire for a Navy career, however, seemed doomed to remain a forlorn hope when in 1908 the nearest he could come to an Annapolis appointment was the position of second alternate. Wishing no one any harm, McDonnell nevertheless could not help hoping that some slight and not too serious disability might remove the two men whose priority made his chances seem hopeless.

Perhaps it was his "lucky" birth date. The first appointee failed to make the entrance grades, illness eliminated the unfortunate alternate, and Eddie McDonnell was on his way to become a Navy man.

At the Naval Academy McDonnell went out vigorously for sports and won his varsity letter in lacrosse and a boxing championship in the 125-pound weight class. He graduated in 1912 and received his commission as Ensign. Then began the Navy's required two years of sea duty. It was while still an Ensign in 1914 that Eddie, as signal officer of a landing force of five men in the occupation of Vera Cruz, received the Congressional Medal of Honor and the citation previously mentioned.

Routine duty aboard ship in peacetime lacked the necessary action for McDonnell, and he determined to get into aviation. There were far more applicants than places, but

Eddie went to the office of Captain Bristol, Director of Naval Aeronautics, determined to "sell" himself, if possible. The McDonnell luck held once more. A man had just been dropped because of faulty eyesight and, though McDonnell was not next on the list, the kudos of his Vera Cruz exploit and his personal salesmanship turned the trick. He was the first in the class of 1912 to be appointed to Naval Aviation.

This was still in the pioneer days of flying. Much to his delight Ensign McDonnell was assigned to work with Orville Wright at Dayton, Ohio. Wright was building a naval plane, and for six weeks McDonnell, as Naval Observer, worked with one of the co-founders of American aviation. From Wright, Eddie learned aerodynamics in the only way possible at the time—by observation, trial and error, and personal instruction. Only three other men were working at the Wright plant. Both engine and plane were built under the watchful eyes of the young Ensign, and while Eddie so far had never been in the air, he was later to fly this very plane at Pensacola, where he was assigned in 1915.

Pensacola was the only naval air base then in existence anywhere in the world. Compared to modern Navy or Army bases, it was primitive indeed. Three large tents served as hangars for two Curtiss planes, only one of which was usually in working order. In February 1915, Ensign McDonnell took his first training flight. Four months later, in June 1915, he took his first solo flight after only ten hours of dual instruction. The long interval between his first

The *Spirit of St. Louis,* equipped with a Wright Whirlwind engine

Wright Aeronautical Corp.

Early two-cylinder Lawrance engine used in Penguin training planes in World War 1

The *China Clipper* (Martin 130) over Golden Gate Bridge

Pan-American Airways

China Clipper on her first scheduled flight across the Pacific, Nov. 22, 1935

Early Sikorsky S-38 amphibian which pioneered the Caribbean in the late 1920's

Juan Trippe receiving Collier Trophy plaque from President Roosevelt in 1937. In the center is Board Chairman Thomas H. Beck of the Crowell-Collier Publishing Co.

Glenn Martin gassing up for his historic flight from Balboa to Avalon in May of 1912

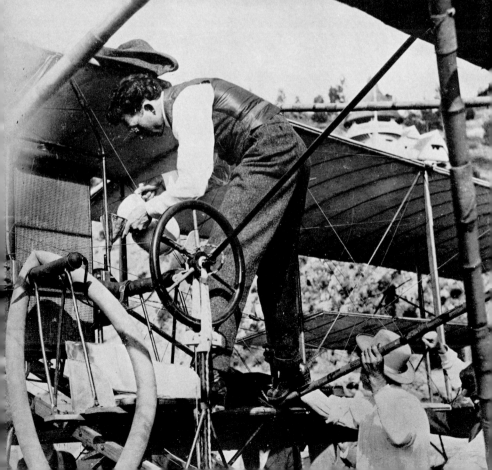

Martin and actress Valeska Surratt after flight at East Newport, Calif., in 1912

Martin (right) and Los Angeles sportsman Frank A. Garbutt with the Martin Model T in 1913

Martin bomber of World War I (note pilot and bombardier in open cockpit)

The Glenn L. Martin Co.

The famed Martin bomber which was the standard of the 1920's, with her
equally famed designers: General Manager Laurence Bell and Chief Engineer
Donald Douglas (extreme left and right). Test pilot Eric Springer stands
second from the left, with Martin next to him

Martin bomber, showing twin Liberty engines, non-retractable four-wheel landing gear, and old-type propellers

Famous transatlantic fliers of the 1920's, partners of the architects of aviation, after lunch at the White House in 1927: (left to right) Lt. Maitland, Chamberlain, Art Goebel, Lindbergh, Ruth Elder, Schlueter, Bronte, Hegenberger, Noville, Byrd, Halderman, Levine, Balchen, and Brock

The Barling bomber of 1921 vintage — a triplane similar to the Caproni triplane

Flight deck of a Pan-American *Atlantic Clipper* today

Type FH-1 aircraft, typical of modern functional design

flight in February and his solo in June was due to his first crash, which occurred in March when his ship lost flying speed, stalled, and dived into the bay, laying Eddie up for a month.

In 1916 McDonnell was the victim of another crash, this time with a freakish twist. He was flying a Burgess-Dunne plane, V-winged and with no tail, possessing an inherent stability. However, in common with most planes of the day, it was underpowered, and in rough air the gust took charge, leaving the pilot little or no control. Eddie had been one of two pilots ordered to Mobile, Alabama, to fly an exhibition for the Mardi Gras celebration. The weather was bad, but thousands of persons who gathered to see the flight had little understanding or interest in what made bad flying weather. So Eddie flew, anyway. A gust of wind threw the ship out of control and it crashed into a three-masted schooner. McDonnell went to the hospital with a hole in his head, but two days later he was flying again.

Soon Eddie became an instructor in flying and aerodynamics, and he then began the design of a new plane.

"All the Navy planes," McDonnell said later, "were too heavy. The Curtiss N-9's then in use were underpowered with their Curtiss OXX motors. My problem was to take that same motor—which was the only one then available—and design a seaplane with pontoons which would give a better performance."

It was something of an assignment, a little difficult to appreciate in present-day aeronautics, with the powerful engines and the modern refinements of design and aeronautical knowledge now available. The planes of that day could just barely fly, in good weather. Lack of power made them stall easily. Yet there was no more powerful motor available.

McDonnell's design was not revolutionary. It was rather a refinement of the existing design. The ship was carefully streamlined to reduce head resistance. Struts that had been all the same sectional size were tapered to the outside edges and made lighter where stresses were less. Yet the modified model had an even higher factor of safety than the old N-9's. In preliminary tests the plane gave even higher performance than equivalent land planes. Existing planes then had a top speed of fifty-five to sixty miles per hour. Eddie's made seventy-five. One hundred fifty feet per minute was the best rate of climb then possible. McDonnell's plane did 300! The plane was in use for some time, and would have been adopted by the Navy except that war was declared and the Navy was unwilling to shift its policies. Besides, European Hispano-Suiza motors, with fifty horsepower more than the OXX, were then made available to America.

Though his design was a success, McDonnell's work was not confined to the laboratory or shop. He served as test pilot at Pensacola in those days, when testing a new plane was an outside gamble with death. But there was more than the search for thrills in McDonnell's test experiences. The knowledge and ability he gained at the controls served him well as first-hand experience on his next assignments and made him as much at home with the joystick as with the slide rule.

During the Pensacola period Major Evans of the Marine Corps essayed a loop-the-loop in a seaplane, becoming the first man in America to perform that hazardous feat. Not to be outdone, Eddie McDonnell, the following day, took up a seaplane and repeated the stunt, the first naval officer to try the tricky evolution.

Throughout his tour of duty at Pensacola, McDonnell's record was an enviable one as an aviator, experimenter, designer, and executive. His contributions furnished a valuable part of the development of early naval aviation. His varied experiences supplied an excellent background for the war duties with which he soon was crowded.

As soon as war was declared, McDonnell was detailed to command and instruct the famous Yale Unit of Naval Aviation. This was a group of young undergraduates from Yale, all young men of means who were operating their own planes. But they were no mere dilettantes, playing with aviation. Under McDonnell they not only learned to fly but did all their own work on the planes as mechanics. The Yale Naval Aviation Unit included such men as Trubee Davison, Harry Davison, Di Gates, and William Rockefeller. Every one of the group who completed training was accepted as a qualified Navy flier and later became fighting and chassé pilots with enviable records. When training was completed, the camp was split up and the men assigned to different units, some going overseas while others distinguished themselves in Coast Patrol work.

McDonnell's wartime work was far from finished. He went to Marblehead and piloted to New London the first

Burgess * twin-motored plane which the Navy had accepted, before reporting as commanding officer of the Hampton Roads naval air station on September 22, 1917. Soon he had brought the station to the front in Navy aviation. One of his achievements at Hampton Roads was the inauguration of the record flight system, which later was adopted at all stations in the service, promoting competitive test flights for distance, duration, and altitude.

In December 1917, McDonnell was sent to France and Italy to inspect the aircraft equipment and manufacturing facilities of those countries with the view of purchasing planes and motors to supplement our own. At Le Croisic, in France, he made his first flight in the war zone, piloting a French seaplane on a long submarine patrol.

His inspection tour occupied him until 1918. During this period he made many test flights of French and Italian planes and learned a great deal of foreign aircraft manufacturing methods. While in Italy, McDonnell secured a temporary assignment to an Italian squadron at Padua. It was here that he earned the Silver Medal for Valor.

McDonnell acted as forward gunner in the plane of the squadron commander. On the night decided upon for the raid the Austrians made a counter-raid upon the Italian airdrome and as McDonnell's machine was wheeled from the hangar the first Austrian bombs landed. A heavy barrage of anti-aircraft fire was sent up and McDonnell's plane took off through anti-aircraft fire of the Italians and

---

* The same Starling Burgess who later became world-famous as co-designer and technical adviser on American Cup Defenders.

bombs of the Austrians. This, too, was night flying, a
highly dangerous job at that time even without the added
menace of enemy bombs and bullets. His plane was the
only one to get off the field.

When they arrived over the German airdrome the
enemy, expecting their own planes' return, threw on the
floodlights, enabling McDonnell and the squadron commander to drop their load of bombs with considerable
damage. It was ascertained later that several returning
German planes had crashed in the bomb craters Eddie's
ship had made. When they returned to their own airdrome
red lanterns had been set out to mark the holes made by
the enemy. "The Italian major stood up in his plane," Eddie
said, "and let loose a stream of what sounded suspiciously
like cussing and ordered another raid in reprisal immediately, since our plane had been the only one to get away
the first time. Just as we were preparing to leave, the Germans and Austrians came over again with another raid!
There were three raids reported that night. They left the
field badly messed up by morning."

During his overseas service McDonnell flew on various
fronts, took part in raids with the British over the submarine base at Bruges, flying Handley Pages and DH-9's,
participated in night and daylight bombing, and more than
once returned with his ship full of holes from machine-gun
and anti-aircraft fire.

In the spring of 1918 he returned to the United States
to organize the northern bombing squadron and in a couple
of months had secured sufficient men and materials to

enable him to sail for France again. As soon as he arrived in Paris he was ordered to go to Milan to take charge of ferrying the Caproni planes across Italy and France to the northern bombing squadrons. He left Milan for Turin as pilot of one of the huge new machines, the first time he had ever been seated at the wheel of the huge triple-engined bomber, and made an historic flight over the Alps. Motor troubles developed during the flight and no less than four motor repairs were made in the air. McDonnell later flew that same plane from Lyons to Calais by way of Paris and then across the English Channel to Eastleigh. He arrived just in time to pilot the first DH-4 from England across the Channel to the northern bombing group.

These are merely a few of the flying highlights of McDonnell's Navy flying career. Before leaving service he found another opportunity to add a "first" to his long list. In Guantanamo Bay, Cuba, he was the first pilot to fly a plane off a battleship without a catapult. A forty-foot runway was built over the gun turret during the winter of 1918–19, and the stunt was planned for the return of the fleet from France. The plane normally took seventy-five feet for a take-off, and the ship was at anchor, giving no aid by running into the wind. In addition, the plane was assembled on the turret platform without plumb bobs or levels, by rule-of-thumb measurement and with no way of knowing whether or not it was properly lined up. Nevertheless, McDonnell's luck or skill—or both—held and the stunt came off successfully.

He left the Navy with the permanent rank of Lieutenant. Shortly afterward he was commissioned a Lieutenant-Commander in the U. S. Naval Reserve, a rank he continued to hold.*

Out of the Navy, he forsook, for the time, his flying adventures, and became Secretary of the Mexican International Corporation, which he later left to join the Kelly-Springfield Motor Truck Company. Here he rose to Vice-President. In 1922 he was Vice-President of R. J. Caldwell Company, Mill Agents, and in 1924 he organized the firm of Smith and McDonnell, a brokerage house.

While with the Mexican International Corporation, McDonnell had met Colonel Grayson M. P. Murphy, a West Pointer who had previously been on the staff of the Rainbow Division. Murphy watched McDonnell's career and became interested in aviation, for which Eddie had still a great interest. The eventual result was that Eddie McDonnell became a partner in the firm of G. M. P. Murphy.

The first aviation venture in the joint financial operations of Murphy and McDonnell was to take a financial interest in Pan American Airways, which was in 1927 seeking to finance its projected Latin American operations. Surveying the situation and guided by his own practical air experiences, McDonnell came to believe in the complete worthiness of the company and its prospects. He realized that an airline in this territory did not have to compete with highly organized and efficient systems of rail transportation. Also Latin American trade was becoming

---

* During World War II he returned to the Navy and attained the rank of Rear Admiral.

increasingly important to the United States. Weather conditions for airline operations seemed nearly ideal, and the only competition was that of slow steamship lines and the ox cart.

Basing his judgment upon these facts, McDonnell advised and assisted in the financing of Pan American. It was at this time that National Aviation Company, Inc. was organized with a capital of three million dollars as an aviation investment trust company. McDonnell, in his capacity as partner with G. M. P. Murphy, subsequently aided in financing such aviation firms as Curtiss-Caproni, United Aircraft, United Airlines, Douglas Aircraft, Lockheed Aircraft, Bell Aircraft, Transcontinental & Western Airlines, and others. National Aviation Company, of which he became President, occupied itself with investing stockholders' money in sound aviation companies. This trust company held representation in the management and on the boards of most of the prominent aviation companies. McDonnell himself became a member of the Board and of the Executive Committee of Pan American Airways. The success of that first venture may be read in the story of Pan American's amazing growth in the years that followed.

The investment trust which McDonnell came to head constantly kept its finger on the pulse of the aviation industry, safeguarding its investments, and tabulating accurate statistics on the comparative operating efficiency of practically every company in the country. At least one high official in the firm traveled frequently over all of the air-transport lines, checked manufacturing facilities and production of all manufacturing companies, and periodically reported the efficiency of performance, economics, and safety measures. By 1938 the firm owned a late-model plane with a cruising speed of seventy-seven miles per hour which McDonnell himself frequently piloted while keeping tab on airline operations.

At that time Eddie McDonnell was reasonably sure the main lines of aviation progress were laid down. Unwilling to set himself up as a prophet, he still looked forward to a steady growth of both commercial and military aviation. One could expect passenger and freight business to increase until a large part of through-passenger business and all first-class mail and express would be carried by air. In time there would be no "air mail" so specified. All transcontinental and transoceanic first-class would be "air mail." On short hauls, whichever medium—air or ground transport—proved the faster would be employed.

This, then, is the story of Eddie McDonnell, conservative investment firm president, expert airman, and private adventure seeker. Still piloting his own plane in later life, McDonnell outgrew the search for aerial thrills and turned to hunting as one of his main diversions. The holder of the Congressional Medal of Honor has been laid up with influenza among the Eskimos at Point Barrow, Alaska, during a polar bear hunt. He has shot mountain sheep and goats in Algeria and Wyoming. He has killed mountain lions in Mexico. He has bagged rhinos and elephants in Africa, returning to London via Imperial Airways, of course, in the first year of that airline's African service.

Never afraid to take a chance personally, yet, where

business and other people's savings were concerned, never one to take foolhardy risks—this is McDonnell, another of those active, farsighted men who took part in early aviation's progress and guided it toward its destiny.

Chapter 10

PAUL REVERE'S HORSE

Charles L. Lawrance

It was the day after the flight
that thrilled the world in 1927 and opened a new epoch in
aviation. Lindbergh's name was on every lip. In all the civi-
lized tongues of the world people were marveling at the
skill and daring of the young pilot who had achieved single-
handed the goal until then a dream—a non-stop transatlantic flight. And in the midst of the tumult and shouting
Charles Lanier Lawrance, builder of the Wright Whirlwind engine that had carried Lindbergh safely to glory,
was asked about the part his brain-child had played in the
flight.

He praised the performance of the man—Lindbergh—
and the importance of the flight, but would make no comment whatsoever on his engine. When pressed for details
he was silent a moment, then said:

"Who remembers Paul Revere's horse?"

This remark became a classic in aviation circles, and the

Wright Whirlwind was sometimes called "Paul Revere's Horse." But more than that, the remark was characteristic of the attitude taken by aeronautical research workers whose unremitting labor helped to make such flights as Lindbergh's possible, and it was typical of Charles Lawrance in particular.

Perhaps another reason why Lawrance rejected the chance to share any part of Lindbergh's glory was the fact that he had attempted to dissuade the young mail pilot from making his Atlantic flight. Six months earlier Lindbergh had approached Lawrance with an offer to buy an airplane which Lawrance and Bellanca had built together. While sympathetic with Lindbergh's aims, Lawrance refused to sell him the plane on the grounds that the flight would be too hazardous, even though the publicity might benefit his engine. As it finally turned out, the Ryan monoplane which Lindbergh later flew—the "Spirit of St. Louis" —was also equipped with the Whirlwind, while the plane which Lawrance had refused to sell was later used by Clarence Chamberlin in his flight to Germany shortly after Lindbergh's hop.

Lawrance's Whirlwind carried other famous flights to glory: Kingsford-Smith across the Atlantic, Byrd to France, and Maitland and Hegenberger from San Francisco to Hawaii, to mention a few. And while Charles Lawrance stoutly denies that he *invented* the first successful air-cooled airplane engine, he is recognized as the man whose careful designs and infinite pains developed it from an inefficient, low-horsepower mechanism to a smooth-running, high-powered, reliable engine.

Lawrance had been tinkering with engines as early as 1901, while he was a student at Yale. He and two class-mates built an automobile when autos were rarities. When the day came to test the finished car the three boys piled in, excitedly started the motor, and put the car in gear. It ran—backward. Lawrance chuckles in the telling of it. "We had made a mistake in the transmission," he said, "and put the bevel gear on the wrong side of the pinion. The result was that we had to put the car in reverse to go forward. And the radiator boiled over on little or no provocation. But it *did* go." In those early days of automotive technology this was about as much as one could ask of any car.

In his senior year he started work on another auto about the time football practice began. He admits that he hated football, but he went out for it because it was something one was expected to do. Then, the very first day of prac-tice, husky, stocky "Charlie" dislocated his knee and had to turn in his uniform. This turn of events left him more time to work on the car, and he went ahead on it with the assistance of a friend, Sidney Breese. In 1905 he graduated and the following year he finished the car. This one ran forward properly.

So far, Lawrance's work with autos had been simply a hobby, the pastime of a young man who found such things interesting. Motherless at the age of ten, he lost his father in his senior year at college. Left to his own counsel, he began to exploit his hobby commercially. The year after his graduation he joined Arthur J. Moulton to build automobiles, and together they turned out twenty-five cars, known as B. L. M.'s. Then come the panic of 1907, and the young firm was wiped out.

Possessing too little capital to risk another venture immediately in the automotive business, young Lawrance went to France to visit his paternal grandparents, who were living there at the time. The family had taken root in America as early as 1635 when the Lawrances settled at Plymouth, Massachusetts, and later at Newton, Long Island. The Laniers, on his mother's side, were descendants of a French Huguenot family of Bordeaux that had settled in the South about the same time.

In France Lawrance found loafing disagreeable. Friends studying at L'Ecole des Beaux Arts in Paris encouraged him to enroll for a course in architecture. He studied there for three years. Motorcars, meanwhile, were no longer treated as curiosities. That was the time of the Pierce-Arrow, the Oldsmobile, the huge Haynes, the Winton, the Mercer, and the Simplex in the United States. The automobile was beginning to progress by leaps and bounds. Ford was soon to build his famous Model T. Yet the industry was in its early stage and in this respect was not far ahead of aviation. Airplanes were still daredevils' scientific toys. Aeronautical science in America was practically nonexistent. Jerome C. Hunsaker was entering M. I. T. as a graduate student for the Naval Construction Corps, and Alex Klemin in London was a graduate electrical engineer uninterested in man's first flights. Glenn Martin in America was one of the few pioneers attempting to build planes.

Charlie Lawrance applied himself to architecture, but could not let automobiles alone. Before his course was completed he had built another car in his spare time. Actually he was never to practice architecture, but the mathematics he learned was of great value to him in his later work. He received his first impetus toward aeronautics by reading Eiffel's classic work (shortly to be translated by Hunsaker), and it so interested him that he made an exhaustive study of aerodynamics. To learn was to build, for Lawrance, and he designed a wing section, known as Eiffel No. 32, in which the center of pressure moved less than any previous design when tested in the Eiffel laboratory in Paris. The practical value of this achievement was demonstrated when a short time later the war broke out. The wing was widely used by both Germans and Allies in airplanes actively engaged in military operations.

But engines still fascinated Charles Lawrance, and his career was beginning to take form as his interests steadily gravitated toward engines and airplanes. He found time amid all his other activities to design and build a 300-horsepower V-type motor before graduating from the Beaux Arts school in 1914, marrying, and returning to America just as war broke out in Europe. It had been an eventful three years. Lawrance returned to America with a wife and the foundation of scientific knowledge he needed for his career.

Back in the United States, he designed an automobile

for a concern that, unhappily, never went into production. He tried his hand also at designing an airplane engine. Finally he bought the assets of a small company which he renamed the Lawrance Aero Engineering Company. Definitely committed now to making airplane engines, he began to draw up a design which had been taking shape in his mind through the years of experimenting with motors. The plans were for an air-cooled airplane engine.

The problem Lawrance had set himself to solve was many-sided. The air-cooled engine, if it could be perfected, would have a number of advantages over the water-cooled engine then in universal use. It would add safety to flight, for there was general agreement throughout the industry that many of the defects which developed in aircraft power plants were due to water-cooling. It would eliminate leaks which forced planes down with annoying frequency. It would remove filters which got out of order. It would solve the problems of storage space and extra weight for carrying water. Weight was a factor so critical that the government was already imposing a stiff penalty on any manufacturer for every pound his finished model exceeded the weight specifications called for in the contract.

Lawrance saw the possibility of devising an air-cooled engine whose parts might be made considerably lighter than those of the typical automotive type engines in general use. If aluminum casting, still in its infancy, could be improved, weight might be lowered appreciably. But Lawrance's proposed engine raised its own, new, mechanical problems. An odd number of cylinders—three or nine

—was required for the type of engine he had in mind, and this posed further difficulties of obtaining parts and materials unlike any then on the market.

His first major problem was one of heat engineering. Simply put, the problem was this: the heavy metal of which conventional cylinders were made required a water-cooling system and a radiator to dispel the heat which the combustion and the moving parts generated. If a lighter, stronger metal could be used and if its material and shape could permit the heat to be dispelled directly into the air, the extra weight of the water and the added air resistance of the radiator could be eliminated. Lawrance decided that cylinders built of highly conductive aluminum could be made to do the trick.

The story which follows demonstrates how experimental research can run a course often contrary to the popular conception of the birth of great inventions or developments. No sudden flash of inspiration revealed a complete and perfect whole. No lucky accident solved a knotty point. Rather an inspired persistence did the job, a painfully slow and patient failure alternated with partial success over and over again. Ignoring the former and heartened by the latter, Lawrance persevered and gradually achieved a more and more practical mechanism.

Ideally, internal combustion engine design is developed and improved by first reducing the cylinders to the lowest possible number which will make a simple, complete unit for testing, and then "whipping the bugs" that inevitably arise in the experimental unit. The more cylinders involved, the more complicated this task becomes. While the perfect unit for developing a new motor would be a single cylinder in which all the factors could be scientifically controlled under laboratory conditions, such a unit is a practical impossibility. Making, therefore, such compromises with practice as ingenuity admitted and circumstances compelled, the Lawrance Aero Engineering Company developed an air-cooled engine of two opposed cylinders. It produced twenty-eight horsepower. This engine met with limited success as a military item.

About this time America entered the war. Lawrance, who was a member of the New York Naval Militia, was kept at work on his engines. The government bought his two-cylinder unit for use in a pilot training plane. This plane became known as the "Penguin," or "Grass-cutter." It had clipped wings and could not actually take to the air, but proved to be of great value in teaching pilots to taxi and take off without doing "ground loops"—that is, nosing the plane over on its back. Ground loops were prevented by placing the Penguin's landing wheels far forward of the center of gravity. The Penguin could, by Lawrance's testimony, be made to jump a fence if properly handled . . . and by a lightweight pilot!

The government put the two-cylinder engines into production with a private manufacturer. Lawrance went on with his experimental work and produced a sixty-horsepower, three-cylinder, air-cooled engine for aircraft designed to be carried on submarines. It was known as Model L and was perfected just about the time of the Armistice.

The Army bought a number of these, and installed them in the Sperry Messenger planes which were employed for messenger service between field units of the Army. A few others were bought by the Navy for their original purpose.

The three-cylinder engine of the Sperry Messenger plane cannot be passed over without recalling the remarkable demonstration Lawrence Sperry, son of the inventor of the gyrocompass, gave to impress the less air-minded officials of Washington. Accustomed to using this type of plane in going from his home in Brooklyn to a Long Island golf course, Sperry made a practical demonstration of the utility of his "air commuter" by landing before the Capitol building at Washington and taxiing up to the steps. Washington officials were impressed, and the spectacular performance obtained desirable publicity for the plane and its engine.

Both during and after the war many obstacles lay in the path of air-cooled engine development. One of the strongest forces of opposition encountered was the inertia that had to be overcome in government circles and in the industry itself. The Curtiss water-cooled OX engine had made possible the flight of most of the airplanes built in America before World War I, and it had proved so dependable in training planes—an estimated ten thousand of our fliers were trained in planes with this type of engine—that there was a general disposition to stick to the proven type. The war produced the miracle of the water-cooled Liberty engine, the first eight-cylinder, finished product being turned over to the Bureau of Standards for testing just thirty-five days after work on the plans and specifications was begun. A twelve-cylinder model followed, and the first production engine of this type was delivered to the government within six months after work had begun on the design *of the eight-cylinder unit.*

In the wake of the war, decreased government appropriations halted mass production of planes and engines and reduced experimental work even while it pushed it to the foreground. Meanwhile, new and remarkable records were set by water-cooled engines. The Model E Hispano-Suiza, for example, underwent a 300-hour, full-power, non-stop test—a grilling trial which amazed even the inner circles of the engineering world, accustomed as they were to achievements of which the general public was often unaware.

Despite these and other remarkable successes of the water-cooled engine, Lawrance was surer than ever of his dream. In the face of repeated discouragement caused by shy capital, inadequate materials, and general skepticism, he set to work on a nine-cylinder air-cooled engine. And this time, too, some officials in Washington were becoming aware of certain basic disadvantages of the water-cooled type for aviation purposes. Encouragement was offered to air-cooled engine designers by the Bureau of Aeronautics of the Navy Department. A 200-horsepower air-cooled type, to replace eventually even the Model E Hispano-Suiza, was asked for. The Lawrance Corporation, working with the Navy Department on this project, developed a nine-cylinder, radial, air-cooled engine known as Model J.

"And this took courage," commented Lawrance in retrospect, reflecting on the vicissitudes of a score of hard-fought years of battling. "The Hispano-Suiza was probably the most reliable engine then in existence and no air-cooled engine could hope to compete with it at once in that respect. Orders were placed, however, and in spite of difficulties the new engine proved its worth to such an extent that some very large orders were placed with my company.

"The Wright Company, seeing their water-cooled engine business diminishing, decided that rather than start an independent air-cooled engine development, they would buy out my company. This was accordingly done and on May 15, 1923, the merger was completed."

That sale netted Charlie Lawrance a half million dollars after ten years' hard work and led two years later to his election as President of the Wright Aeronautical Corporation.

Just before the merger took place F. B. Rentschler, former President of Wright, and George J. Mead, former Chief Engineer of Wright, decided to form a new engine corporation: the Pratt & Whitney Aircraft Company. They developed after intensive work their Wasp model, rated at 425 horsepower. It was used in the Navy for observation and pursuit planes, and its success in competition with water-cooled engines in the United States led to its adoption for commercial transportation. The air-cooled engine was proving to be worth the investment it required.

Lawrance had worked with the Army in its experimental research at McCook Field in Dayton and while there had met a British consulting metallurgical engineer, S. D. Heron. He had also met an American, E. T. Jones, who had been carrying on a series of experiments in the design of cylinder heads for an air-cooled engine. He succeeded in arranging for their services with the Wright Company. Heron, like Lawrance, had considerable background of practical shop training, as well as some experience abroad with experimental air-cooled engines. He also possessed a patience that matched that of Lawrance.

The three men went to work to "whip the bugs" in the radial nine-cylinder design which Lawrance was determined to perfect. The enterprise and its problems were neither new nor radical. The British had launched several radial air-cooled engine projects that strove ambitiously for a unit of 400 horsepower, but no satisfactory results were obtained before the Armistice. One of the obstacles was the lower efficiency and greater fuel consumption of the air-cooled as compared to the liquid-cooled engine. Air-cooled engines had been built. Some of them worked. But as yet no one had built one that could compete on equal terms of efficiency and dependability with the liquid-cooled engine—no one until Lawrance and his associates.

He studied flame propagation in the cylinder, spark gaps, piston throw, lubrication, and all the thousand and one details that go into the design of a successful gas engine. One by one, the "bugs" were eliminated as the engine drew nearer to completion.

Finally came the crowning success for which Lawrance had worked so hard and long, with the pertinacity, vigor, and sense of team play which characterized him. His achievement gains in its recounting through his own modest statement:

"The researches and experiments at Dayton, covering a period of years, were very comprehensive in character and showed some very remarkable results. Mr. Jones became chief engineer of the Wright Company, and it was decided to redesign the former Lawrance nine-cylinder engine, then known as the Wright J-4 B, taking advantage of the experience of Jones and Heron in air-cooled cylinder design.

"The new engine was known as the J-5, or 'Whirlwind.' Its power was no greater than before, but the specific fuel consumption was about as low as any water-cooled aviation motor built then. It was thus remarkably suited as a power plant for the extraordinary series of trans-Atlantic and trans-Pacific flights which characterized the year 1927 and which turned the minds of the whole world to the possibilities of flying.

"With those epoch-making flights, in my opinion, the science and industry of aviation turned the corner from poverty to success, and the ultimate future of aviation in the United States became as assured as the future of the automobile industry."

He left the Wright Company in the spring of 1929 to become the Vice-President of Curtiss-Wright, where he remained until the autumn of 1930, when he formed his own Lawrance Engineering Research Company to design and experiment with newer, more powerful engines that would give the performance he foresaw airplanes of the future would demand.

By then the Whirlwind had become established as the premier and pioneer air-cooled engine of the air. Over many skyways its powerful drone marked the safe, swift passage of mail planes, airliners, and military aircraft. As a result honor and recognition came increasingly to the man who so modestly provided "Paul Revere's Horse" and played a vital role in a revolution of the aircraft engine industry which was not to be repeated until the jet airplane appeared.

Charlie Lawrance, at fifty, could have leaned back and rested upon his laurels, satisfied with a hard job well done. Like many another pioneer, however, he could not rest, He did not seek the acclaim and credit which came to him. Fame left him as it found him, genial, ruddy, boyish, apt to turn up at some aviation conference in a sack suit not too snugly tailored, friendly and unassuming, and still enthusiastically hard at work.

Chapter 11

GLOBE GIRDLER

Juan Terry Trippe

In August 1937, the Collier Trophy was awarded to Pan American Airways. The service was not ten years old, yet this award was perhaps one of the most deserved since Robert Collier first presented the famous statuette for "the greatest achievement in aviation in America, the value of which has been demonstrated in use or practice during the preceding year."

The Collier Trophy was awarded to Pan American Airways, but as an organization may be the lengthening shadow of a man, so may it be said that the trophy was awarded in reality to Juan Terry Trippe, affable, suave, farsighted, young (then thirty-eight) guiding genius of the world's largest airline. In a few years he had built Pan American's far-flung empire of the air until it spanned fifty-two thousand miles of scheduled airways. He had girdled South America against the established competition of France and Germany, linked the West Indies to the American continents, and effected a tie-in with the National Airline of China which gave him a forty-five per cent financial interest in its affairs, to the consternation of Europe. He had built airports on forgotten coral isles in the remote Pacific and established regularly scheduled transportation halfway around the globe to China. And at the time the award was given in 1937, Pan American was making the first test flights and expanding its organization to extend regular transport service across the North Atlantic.

It was the custom for European airlines to be liberally subsidized by their governments, but the United States Government extended only partial, indirect subsidies in the form of mail contracts. Apart from these and without sharing in the $68,000,000 our domestic airways had received from the Department of Commerce, Pan American was planned and built by private enterprise. By 1937 it had surpassed the government-subsidized airlines of Europe. It had the highest percentage of completed schedules, the most effective radio communication system, and the fewest fatal accidents of any air transport system extant. This, then, was the world-girdling achievement of Juan Terry Trippe and his associates in less than a decade.

In the beginning, in 1928, throughout the thirty-nine countries and colonies covered by Pan American's air network ten years later, there were practically no airports, no emergency landing fields, no beacons, no radio service. Only four weather stations were in operation, the Cuban at Havana, the United States stations at Puerto Rico and the Canal Zone, and the Mexican station at Mexico City. All those aids to our domestic airlines which were supplied by local and federal government assistance, Pan American had to make for itself, even at the North American terminals in Miami, Florida; Brownsville, Texas; and Los Angeles, California.

That Pan American was able to surmount such obstacles is due especially to the earlier experiences of its president, Juan Trippe. He began his amazing career under what, according to the conventional rags-to-riches formula, was an extraordinary handicap. He was not a product of the slums, nor did he lift himself by sheer determination and his bootstraps from poverty. Instead, Juan Trippe was the son of a New York banker, certainly not rich by Wall Street standards, yet comfortably well off. He was a descendant of seventeenth-century Marylanders and seagoing Yankees. His forebears on the paternal side include a sea hero and an admiral. From his mother Juan inherits a leavening of Spanish influence—his name being given him in memory of a great-aunt, Juanita Terry, who married his uncle, a pioneer of Venezuela.

Trippe has acquired the reputation of being a man of mystery because of a passion for personal anonymity where the achievements of Pan American are concerned. While this role has undoubtedly been of service in assisting him to pursue the quiet, swift course of action he habitually has taken, it is not assumed. A trait of reticence has distinguished him at least since his school days at Yale. There he earned a reputation for shyness while early manifesting his tremendous capacity for work. He was editor of the *Record*, played football, and did considerable flying for those days, all the while keeping up with his schoolwork. He was quiet most of the time, he was usually tremendously busy, and he concentrated on work rather than student politics or social life. Those were reflections of attitudes he was to carry into later life.

When the United States went to war in 1917, Juan joined the Naval Reserve Flying Corps and emerged at the end of hostilities with an Ensign's wings. After his return to Yale he organized the first collegiate flying club there. Yet when he graduated he followed the traditional occupation of many another Yale graduate at the time: selling bonds. Securities, however, could not still the roar of airplane engines in young Trippe's ears. Shortly, he abandoned bonds, purchased several surplus wartime planes, and organized Long Island Airways, of which he was president, traffic manager, dispatcher, pilot, and not infrequently mechanic and hangar sweeper. Long Island Airways spent most of its time ferrying the fashionable about Long Island Sound and locality. It is interesting to note that Long Island Airways was one of the first "fixed base" services in the country; aerial transport previously was confined almost wholly to chartering a private plane to travel from one rare and not-too-convenient airport to a second rare and specified airport. It is also interesting to note that Long Island Airways lost money. Trippe did not ignore the lesson.

Then in 1925 the new Kelly Air Mail Act offered indirect subsidies to air-mail carriers. Trippe saw his opportunity, and enthusiastically persuaded several of his friends who had belonged to the college aero club to help him finance an airline from New York to Boston. They merged with another firm that was being organized and formed Colonial Air Transport, while Trippe sped to Washington, bid for, and was awarded the New York–Boston air-mail contract. This time he was fairly launched upon his career of air transport operation.

The New York–Boston run did not satisfy Trippe. He was determined to transport people as well as mail. When, in this same year, the Dutch engineer Anthony Fokker came to America with the first important three-engine plane, the wooden Fokker trimotor, Trippe was enthusiastic about the design. He saw it as the inevitable solution to the problem of engine failure and immediate forced landing. To the future president of Pan American, conviction meant action. He visualized the New York–Boston run lengthening, stretching down the East coast to Florida and jumping off for points south. John Hambleton and Cornelius Vanderbilt "Sonny" Whitney shared his ambitious ideas. Colonial Air Transport must purchase several trimotors and extend its operations!

But when this plan was laid before the board of directors, a conservative majority blocked it. Startled, perhaps, by the magnitude of the proposed operations, they shook their heads and signified they were content to continue operating between New York and Boston. The eventual result was that Trippe, Hambleton, and Whitney liquidated their holdings, withdrew from Colonial, and formed a new company.

The new venture, a holding company at first, called itself Aviation Corporation of the Americas. Trippe was practically the "poor boy" among the backers, who included Hambleton, "Sonny" Whitney, Grover Loening, W. Averill Harriman, William H. Vanderbilt, Sherman M. Fairchild, John Hay Whitney, William Rockefeller, Seymour Knox, and Edward O. McDonnell—the same Eddie McDonnell whose story is told in another chapter and who in 1927 was just beginning his partnership with the G. M. P. Murphy Company. The aim of the new corporation was to buy into existing air enterprises and to bid on whatever air-mail contracts might come along. Assuming that their bids would be successful, Trippe hired as operations man a fellow countryman of Fokker's (whom Fokker had introduced to him) and a brilliant engineer in his own right, André Priester.

Here is an example of Pan American's methods that produced subsequent success. The group surrounding Trippe, Hambleton, and Whitney was made up almost wholly of men who were pilots themselves, men who were familiar with the airplane and its operation. Also, they were men of means and need not bother with bankers who would be more familiar with the operation of the stock market than of an airline. Trippe was taking no chance of repeating those events which compelled him to yield to conservative opinion in his previous venture. Finally, a sort of practical idealism, hard to describe, permeated the group and gave to the enterprise a persistent glowing zeal that proved as essential as the breath of life in bringing to pass the startling, swift developments that were to amaze the air transport world during the years of the Great Depression.

Early in 1927 Trippe learned that the government planned to extend air-mail service from Florida to Cuba. His firm was not the only one interested. Two others were already in the field, and in July one of them obtained the contract. While negotiations to bring about a merger proceeded, Trippe visited Cuba and obtained exclusive landing rights which effectively grounded his competitors. Finally, in October, the three firms merged and took the name of Pan American Airways Corporation, an operating subsidiary of the larger holding company, Aviation Corporation of the Americas.

An immediate obstacle presented itself. The contract called for service to begin by October 19, 1927. When the merger was completed a half-month before the deadline no flying equipment was on hand, although Trippe and his friends, with the foresight that henceforth characterized their operations, had gone to work on operations problems while the more financial-minded members were still concerned with the financial details of the merger. Trippe and the others collected a skeleton personnel, ordered three Fokker trimotors, purchased a mud flat in Key West, and began converting it into a landing field. Passenger stations and hangars remained to be built. Maritime clearance regulations, which had never before applied to airplane operations, had not been arranged for. The Post Office Department, disgusted with previous delays in the Caribbean, refused to grant an extension of time. A seemingly hopeless task stretched before the new firm. It found itself facing the desperate necessity of meeting the contract and saving the whole financial structure that had been so painfully put together.

This was Trippe's first experience with a type of situation he has since coped with in a manner that has characterized his entire career: taking fast, forced moves and expanding facilities with little or no time to digest the experience gained in previous moves.

But in this instance there had been no previous moves. To create an entire airline, complete to passenger stations, runways, and maintenance equipment by October 19 was manifestly impossible. Nevertheless, when the deadline arrived a rented plane was flown the ninety miles from Key West to Havana and then returned, fulfilling the terms of the contract. Less than a month after the birth of the new company regular operations began, on October 28, with the pioneer ocean flier Edwin C. Musick at the controls of one of the new Fokkers, the same "Uncle Ed" Musick who later flew the China Clipper on the first scheduled transpacific flight, the same Captain Ed Musick who was to lose his life over that same Pacific when his plane mysteriously exploded on an experimental cruise.

So Pan American Airways came into existence—and immediately began to expand. Early in 1928 Trippe announced to his associates—later they learned to be ready for such surprises—that they would extend their airline as fast as possible to the shores of South and Central America. Early the following year routes were opened to Puerto Rico and the Canal Zone from Florida, and to Mexico City from Texas.

That Trippe's tactics were the right tactics to use became evident when country after country was won over to his propositions. It became increasingly apparent to the United States Department of State that Trippe was building more than an airline. Each of his sleek ships was an emissary of American prestige and good will. Each landing field built for his commercial purposes was a potential air base for hemisphere military defense, if need be. A reserve of valuable flight experience was accumulating toward the same end.

Nor were the services of Pan American limited to furnishing transportation by air. It soon was evident that the airline offered uniquely more to Americans at home and abroad and to the inhabitants of the various countries themselves. If a tropical storm knocked out an electric communication system Pan American's own radio station remained as a co-operative link with the outside world. If Pan American had no station in that particular place it could and did dispatch a plane with a fifty-watt transmitter to reestablish touch with the stricken area. Companies wanting to sell their products in any countries served by Pan American received from the airline all necessary data on prices, competitors, politics, or consumption, as well as suggestions on the best way to develop the market.

Pan American's "hurricane watch" has saved American taxpayers incalculable dollars. It has not been entirely an altruistic gesture, of course. Necessity demanded that the airline establish a chain of weather stations around the Caribbean shores where the big winds spring up. Nevertheless, the co-operation of these stations with the Weather Bureau has saved money and lives in the charting of big storms' progress. While Trippe's policies of courtesy and friendly dealing might be called merely a good way to win business, without them the United States might now find herself involved in less South American trade and enjoying considerably less national good will from South American neighbors.

The China situation was another typical example of Trippe policy, which when further analyzed becomes that of never taking a chance if possible. His early espousal of the multi-motored plane followed this principle. His mail policies were built upon the same basis, except that instead of eliminating motor failure as the element of chance he eliminated the possible vagaries of nationalist policies, depended upon his own staff and equipment, ready and working, rather than upon a contractual arrangement with separate airlines. Nothing less than a unified air service under his control would suffice.

In China the concession of a landing field was impossible. In order to keep the Japanese from establishing an airline on Chinese soil, all other powers had been excluded as well. As long ago as 1930–31 Trippe had foreseen that the Pacific would soon be flown—which is another way of saying that he intended to span it. He had dispatched Richard C. Long to Portugal to negotiate a contract allowing Pan American to land in Macao, the spot that had been selected as the best possible landing place since the British refused to open Hong Kong. Again there was no magic in the deal, except the magic of long-distance planning. When the Clipper planes were ready for the hop the details had long been arranged. The British had even opened Hong Kong rather than allow Macao to begin to compete as an air trade center. Similar foresight prevailed in the Atlantic crossings. Pan American arranged for its landing permits in Ireland in 1930, *six years before* any other company even attempted negotiations.

In April 1935, the first series of test flights to Hawaii began, an overwater jump of 2410 miles. This was the longest scheduled flight of its kind in the world, longer by five hundred-odd miles than the Atlantic hop. The next jump, to Midway Island, is 1380 miles, then 1252 miles to Wake Island, 1560 miles to the Philippines, and the final jump of 759 miles to Macao. Seven years of planning and study had gone into the girdling of the Pacific by air. The 500-mile hop from Kingston, Jamaica, to Barranquilla, Colombia, had become known as the "Atlantic Laboratory" where Trippe trained his personnel, tested equipment, and seasoned operating executives.

Early in 1935 the ship "North Haven" sailed from San Francisco with five complete dismantled "air bases" in her hold as well as tractors, food, radio towers, Diesels, and two ten-ton electric generators. There were over a million separate items in all, assembled on paper by Pan American planning engineers, ready to be fitted together by the modern pioneers going forth to temporary exile. Four months to the day, the "North Haven" was back in San Francisco, newly erected air bases dotting the Pacific behind her. And in August of the same year a Sikorsky S-42 flew as far as Wake Island. In October it flew to Guam, and in November the first new Martin ship, the China Clipper, arrived on the West coast and was flown the entire distance to Manila. A sidelight on the safe performance of those ships was the fact that the second Martin ship, the Philippine Clipper, flew the whole trip and returned in December, logging 1000 miles of the return trip on only three of its four engines. In July 1936, the whole distance to Manila was scheduled for mail and express service and three months later was opened for passenger service.

Throughout its comparatively brief career Pan American Airways has pioneered, rapidly enlarging the scope and distances of its flights as fast as improving equipment would permit. In its airplanes Pan American has steadily demanded of builders—as in the case of the Martin Clippers, Boeing Clippers, Lockheed Constellations—performance far exceeding that of existing equipment, and has gotten it. Equally of his personnel and executives, Juan Trippe has demanded the nearly impossible in administration—and has gotten it.

Trippe is not the blustering bully type of leader, nor does he inspire his associates by oratory or pep talks. Quiet, considerate, and mild-spoken, he nevertheless has the knack of asking for a certain job that seems impossible and then, when superhuman work has made it reality, instead of dwelling upon the achievement with fulsome praise he nods and goes on to the next "impossible" that is waiting. Indeed, once he has laid out a plan of action, no matter how remote are the possibilities of its completion within the time he has allotted, he speaks of it thenceforth as though it were already accomplished. And it invariably becomes so.

What is the inspiration of the hard-working young men in Pan American's service? There certainly are no "soft jobs" in the organization. The remuneration in the '30's was small compared to jobs of similar responsibility in other companies, for Trippe believes in high pay for flying personnel and relatively less pay for executives.

"Pan Am's" representatives abroad are not merely average businessmen. They are outstanding, secure in the knowledge that though there may be no easy money in their jobs they have good jobs—careers in a thrilling, world-wide enterprise akin to the British diplomatic service tradition. They have been lifted above mere jobholding executive positions, just as Trippe's flying personnel have been lifted above the status of "air chauffeurs."

On the mechanical side Pan American has had to originate entirely new equipment for its overseas pioneering. Hugo C. Leuteritz, Pan American communications engineer, largely invented and developed the special 2000-mile radio direction finder that was put into use on the Caribbean and Pacific flights. The usual radio equipment of domestic airlines was valueless on the long voyages of the Clippers. A radio range beam would not carry such distances, nor would existing two-way radio equipment. Under Leuteritz's direction, new equipment was designed that was unique among airlines.

For training of flying personnel a rigorous program was incorporated into the system of flight operations in the decade of the 1930's. The details were worked out by André Priester, who met Trippe back when the New York–Boston run was the extent of his operations. The training placed safety first in the mind of every flight officer from the newest Apprentice Pilot (who was required to be a university graduate to begin with and to hold a transport license) through Junior Pilot, Flight Engineer, Senior Pilot, and Master of Ocean Aircraft.

As the program was worked out, before the Apprentice Pilot—already an expert flier—can become a Junior Pilot he learns traffic communications, meteorology, how to help the radio officer, mechanics, etc. As Junior Pilot he must become also a licensed engine mechanic, licensed airplane mechanic, licensed radio operator, and celestial navigator. He must know traffic problems along the route he flies. He must have passed examinations in international clearances, international law, maritime law, one language, and seamanship. At the end of all that he will be eligible for position of second officer. (This was the junior officer post on a Pan American flying boat before the war.)

The Flight Engineer specializes further on radio and engines, and the Senior Pilot adds to all this many hours of experience in the air and in overwater flying to qualify him further as Captain of the ship, Pan American's planes being run after the manner long tested by nautical tradition. Such unequaled, exhaustive training of flying personnel is instrumental in accounting for Pan American's negligible accident rate.

These features of Trippe's organization are not the only ones. The phenomenal growth of Pan American Airways which has taken place—and of which this chapter recounts only the pioneering decade—can be traced to several factors, the most important of which is probably Juan Trippe's super-strategic technique in planning and building his world-girdling operations. It is a technique which has baffled many because they could not reconcile it with Trippe's deceptive personality.

Amiable, bland, smooth-shaven, firm, seemingly inscrutable on the outside, and impelled within by a driving ambition and earnestness to pursue with extraordinary tenacity the paths to air empire, Juan Trippe has been the subject of considerable speculation. His "system" which has produced such amazingly successful results has been variously described as diabolical cunning, high-pressure lobbying, graft, or a mysterious leverage within the State Department that has made his airline virtually an independent instrumentality of the government.

But reduced to essentials his procedure has consisted in sending out engineers, explorers, and legal men, frequently possessing State Department training, to survey the territory—political and legal as well as physical—over which he proposed to begin operations. From them he learned just what a particular government's requirements would be if service were established across national borders, and what service would be most valuable commercially. Finally, he secured all necessary options, concessions, and franchises that might be required for the successful operation of an efficient air service. The secret, if secret there be, lay in preparing the ground so thoroughly in advance, and in demonstrating so vividly that Pan American offered a genuine service without exploitation of the territory, that the country in question would recognize no other airline was nearly so well equipped to handle the business or render those services. It was, simply, farsighted preparation plus tactful handling and shrewd bargaining plus efficient service. These factors, consistently and intelligently administered under Trippe's direction, made an unbeatable combination. Other lines might consider obtaining the same concessions, buying the same equipment, bidding on the same mail contracts, only to find that Trippe had considered the possibilities earlier, acted upon them, and was ready to offer immediate service. In 1926, before Pan American was organized, Trippe visited Alaska. Six years later he started regular service there, and insistently practical, ordered systematic investigation begun on arctic weather and flying conditions. That same year he bought into a Chinese airline, foreseeing it as a link in a future transpacific service. The year the Collier Trophy was awarded Pan American, 1937, Trippe obtained exclusive landing rights in Portugal, although adequate equipment delayed starting regular service until over a year later. These examples are typical of Trippe's farsighted planning.

Juan Terry Trippe, a modern empire builder, is a far

cry from the American pioneers who hacked, swore, and cudgeled what they wanted from a frontier country. Juan Trippe's way has been different: it has been infinitely more subtle in crossing the last frontiers of an air empire and far less productive of the unfortunate repercussions and dislocations that so often accompany swift readjustment. The leader of his group, rather than its boss, Trippe said when presented the Collier Trophy that,—"he accepted it not for himself—but the 4900 men of his team." And that is as close an approximation of Pan American's spirit as any.

Chapter 12

MASTER BUILDER

Glenn L. Martin

When Pan American Airways announced in 1931 that it was in the market for airplanes of unprecedented size and cruising range—flying boats of a non-stop range of 2500 miles and averaging with a pay load better than 120 miles an hour against a thirty-mile head wind—designers wouldn't listen. Such requirements called for more in airplane performance than ever had been incorporated in one design. Engineers all agreed it couldn't be done.

Almost all, that is. Glenn L. Martin thought he could do it, and Martin from long experience had a way of getting things done. He submitted a bid, was accepted, and set to work.

Four years later, in November 1935, Captain Ed Musick lifted the first of the huge, new, Martin-built China Clippers from the waters of San Francisco Bay and headed toward Manila on the first scheduled flight of Pan American's Pacific service. The sleek air monster under Musick's control marked a new achievement in ocean flying. More than half its gross weight of 51,000 pounds was *useful load*, instead of the customary one-third or less. It carried a crew of seven and, in addition to regular aerial equipment, such nautical items as an anchor and winch, lifeboats and lifebelts, bilge pump, complete galley with icebox, grill, sink, and dishes. It provided comfortable sleeping accommodations for from sixteen to thirty passengers, depending upon the length of the hop and the resultant amount of fuel that must be carried. Its 3600 horsepower was equal to a big railroad locomotive. Its length of over ninety feet made it larger than Columbus' "Pinta."

This, then, is the ship that Martin built, along with two others like it for the same run. It was a far cry from the days when the following item appeared in the Los Angeles *Times* in the summer of 1910:

SANTA ANA, August 4th. Glenn L. Martin of this city is reported to have been up in the air a half dozen times in a biplane just completed by him. . . . He has equipped his outfit with a 15 horsepower Ford auto motor.

A model of that biplane was to stand in after years on a desk in Glenn Martin's office, looking impossibly fragile in its cloth-and-bamboo construction. It seems unbelievable that man could have entrusted himself to the air in such man-killing, experimental box kites. But Martin not only built them—he flew them himself, rating for years among such pioneer aviators as Glenn Curtiss, Lincoln Beachey, Brookins, and Robinson.

To draw a momentary comparison of theory with practice, if Alexander Klemin, first director of the Guggenheim School of Aeronautics, were cast in the role of an Einstein of aviation, then Glenn Martin would be perhaps its Edison. Klemin—the mathematical wizard who could never become a good pilot himself—worked with figures and formulas. Drawing upon his exhaustive theoretical knowledge of mathematics and aerodynamics, he made airplanes grow on paper that were safe in the air.

Glenn Martin, however, was flying his man-made contraptions before there was such a thing as an aviation school, by the direct process of building the planes and taking them into the air.

"A good aviator," he said once, with almost shy humor in a country-boy way never quite outgrown, "was considered someone who could walk away from a wreck." And reckoning the terrific mortalities among fliers in that past era, the remark is more tragic than amusing.

Thus, on one occasion in 1911 during Martin's barnstorming days, he was doing some low exhibition flying when suddenly he noticed another pilot approaching in a steep forty-five degree glide. "I thought something must be wrong. The pilot seemed to have gone crazy. Then, as the plane passed me, I saw his body hanging limp at the controls. Just what had happened to him no one will ever know, for a moment later the ship crashed to earth."

Martin landed and helped extricate the body of the other

pilot. It was a ghastly sight. The body was badly broken and some of the bones were protruding from the flesh. Within the next half hour another plane crashed, killing its pilot, and Martin was again among those who pulled the pilot's body from the splintered wreckage. Then he took off in his own ship and made an altitude record for the day.

So Glenn Martin's knowledge of aircraft was accumulated in the practical school. Without benefit of higher mathematics or aerodynamics he was building planes since early youth. Added to this practical knowledge was an intuitive *feeling* for the right thing in plane construction that proved invariably baffling to his engineering staff, yet was unerringly right. Martin always depended in part upon that intuitive sense. When a new design would be brought to him for approval he would glance over the drawings that had been worked out by the engineering department. Without recourse to figures or formulae, he might run his finger accusingly over one detail.

"This won't do. It's wrong! You shouldn't bring me a thing like this. Fix it."

Elaborate calculation or experiment would demonstrate the truth of what Martin had instinctively felt. The one point he criticized *was* wrong—and it was fixed.

Glenn L. Martin was born in Macksburg, Iowa, in 1886. His father, Clarence Y. Martin, was manager of the Macksburg hardware store and he planned a career for young Glenn in the same business. The project did not meet with his son's entire approval. Young Glenn was an inveterate kite flier and constructor. Long before the Wrights' first flight in 1903 he was building kites which possessed automatic stability and was selling them to other youngsters at twenty-five cents each. This juvenile industry was not particularly profitable, but it did enable him to put the returns back into building more kites, a principle which he has consistently followed ever since.

His first job was with an auto agency in Kansas where he worked on the old 4½-horsepower Oldsmobile cars. Gas engines fascinated him. He soon became an excellent mechanic. At about the same time came the news that the Wrights had stayed in the air for one minute and forty seconds, and Glenn did not rest until he had seen this miracle for himself. Afterward, he told his mother:

"I can build one of those! Shucks, it's nothing but a kite with an engine in it."

There were no textbooks on airplane engineering, no schools. But someone else had flown. He decided that he would also.

In 1909 the Martins, father and son, were operating a garage in Santa Ana, California. At night, after his work was finished, Glenn worked on his first plane, by rule of thumb and his knowledge of kites and gas engines. There were few parts he could buy. He had to make them himself. Doggedly, night after night in the lamplight, Martin worked on his plane.

Those were the days when a man who wanted to fly was considered more than a little crazy and the elder Martin looked with no favor on his son's idiosyncrasy. His mother, however, stifled whatever qualms she had over her son's safety, realizing as she did his complete absorption in aircraft, and stimulated him with her encouragement and confidence. It was her hand that held the lamp while Glenn worked and her undeviating affection through all the early years that spurred him on.

In August of 1909 Martin took his first plane to the flat California mesa nearby. Alone in the late-afternoon twilight, he spun the propeller, sat in the little bucket seat on the lower wing, stretched his feet out to the rudder bar before him in space . . . and flew!

His fate was sealed, then. All his energies and all his money went into building planes. The first had been a biplane. He began work on a monoplane. Meanwhile, in December 1910, the local newspapers heralded an exhibition flight in his biplane under the auspices of the Santa Ana Merchants and Manufacturers Association, at McFadden's pastures. The Pacific Electric car line ran special cars to and from the field so that all might witness the new miracle. Schools in the locality dismissed their classes "so that pupils may witness the exhibition. It will be the kind of thing that may not be seen here again for a long time"—to quote one of the newspaper stories of the day.

The flight was successful. Three thousand persons were thrilled by the young aviator's skill. In the words of another paper, "He flew southwards for about a mile and circled in a space remarkably short for aeroplane work."

Martin continued making exhibition flights, working all the while on his monoplane. Later in December he tried it out. On the initial flight, however, the wind lifted one wing when he was only two feet above the ground, and he crashed. He was not seriously injured, and for the next few years he continued building new planes with the profits of each summer season's barnstorming flights.

Of all the flying pioneers of that day Glenn Martin was one of the leading lights, but with one difference. While many men were flying bravely and risking their necks for the sheer love of the game, Martin had a deeper purpose. He was a daring, fearless flier. At one meet at Dominguez Field he took all the prizes offered in his class, more than Glenn Curtiss, Brookins, or Robinson. He broke several altitude records of his day. He carried a passenger when that meant the passenger had to ride astride a beam behind the pilot. He made one of the first flights in darkness with Lincoln Beachey and Howard Gill, bombing an imaginary fort. In short, he did all the things that other well-known pilots of the day were doing, including a few ideas of his own. But Martin's basic and dominating urge was to build planes. The profits of exhibition flying were not inconsiderable. He would return from a season of barnstorming with upwards of twenty-five thousand dollars. And that would immediately go into new planes he was building for himself and other fliers. As early as 1911 the newspapers were referring to him as "the well-known aeronautical operator, teacher and manufacturer."

The tide changed in 1913 when Martin sold his first plane to the United States Government. He then quit his exhibition flying and devoted himself wholly to manufacturing and testing his own ships. In 1915 he began to consider relocating in the East, where skilled labor and materials were most available.

Martin's planes at this time were among the most advanced in aeronautical design. He had not, however, developed his own engine. The Wright Company, on the other hand, had an engine but not a particularly efficient plane. A business merger was effected, and the Wright-Martin Company of New York was formed in the fall of 1916. The plan was to use the Wright engine in the Martin plane, which had demonstrated the superiority of wing ailerons over the Wrights' original method of warping the entire wing.

About the time of the merger America entered the First World War. The new company purchased the old Simplex automobile plant, which was one of the best machine shops in the country, and turned to war production. The Wright engine soon was found to be too low-powered for warplane performance. Under franchise they manufactured the European-designed Hispano-Suiza motors for the Allies. But Martin chafed under the fact that they continued only as motor manufacturers. The Martin plane had been sidetracked. Despite the fact that all his resources were tied up in the Wright-Martin Company he engineered at that time one of the most decisively daring moves of his career. He resigned from the Wright-Martin Company to set up for himself.

He had no resources, no backing, nothing but his own ideas and the determination to build planes. The first problem was: where?

After making a careful survey of the country he settled upon Cleveland as the logical spot for a plant which still had no more substantial reality than a dream—a dream that he rapidly set about realizing. In Cleveland he found himself quite alone, with no friends or prospects, a young man out to start an airplane factory. His method was characteristically direct. He looked through the Cleveland Blue Book and selected the names of twelve of the city's financial leaders, with Mr. Samuel Mather at the head of the list. Martin sold him the idea first, then approached eleven other "crowned heads" of Cleveland, and the Glenn L. Martin Company of Cleveland was launched.

By this time World War I was nearing its end. In the early days after America's entrance, the Army considered adopting the British Handley Page bomber and the Italian Caproni, on which comparative tests were made by Lieutenant H. R. Harris, later chief test pilot at McCook Field. Neither of these planes was officially adopted. Instead, contracts were let for the Martin bomber, designed by Donald Douglas and powered with two Liberty engines. The Armistice in 1918 prevented this new, huge, biplane bomber from seeing action, although its tests promised it superiority over any bombers then in the air.

During the latter months of the war and shortly afterward, the Martin Company developed for the Navy a converted Martin bomber capable of carrying and launching a torpedo. The company also developed one or two experimental Martin transport planes modified to carry a machine-gun crew and equipment for guerrilla warfare, such as the expeditions in Mexico entailed.

In the early years in Cleveland, Martin had in his employ many who later became leading executives and designers in aviation. Among them were Laurence Bell, who set up Bell Aircraft in Buffalo, and Donald Douglas, since highly successful at the head of his own company in California.

A story that is an interesting sidelight on Martin's way of doing things is told of the time when both Bell and Douglas were working at the Martin plant. Douglas was at the time Martin's Chief Engineer, Bell was Factory Manager. The two men held bitterly opposing views on a subject that had come up, and it seemed impossible to arbitrate or compromise their conflicting opinions.

Martin considered the matter and decided that in this case Bell was in the right. Douglas, however, held out. "If this is going to be done Bell's way," he said, "I'm leaving." Bell was perhaps less vitally important to the plant at that time than was Douglas, whose brilliant designs had contributed largely to some of Martin's most successful planes. But at the ultimatum, Martin looked up at him mildly.

"Well," he said, "if you feel that way about it, Doug, I guess there's nothing else for you to do." And Douglas left, a move which in this instance did not react to his disadvantage.

Martin manufactured in Cleveland for twelve years. During and after the war he enjoyed a period prosperous enough to enable him to buy out his backers. The officers in the Air Corps held him in high esteem as an honest manufacturer, a progressive designer, and one who could be depended upon to carry out Army specifications to the letter. In later years he built many planes for the government, including pursuit ships and dive bombers for the Navy. With increasing business each year he felt the lack of any waterway for launching hydroplanes and flying boats. Also, his Cleveland site, wisely chosen, had so risen in value that it was too valuable to use as a factory site. A move was again indicated.

In 1928, then, as he was finishing up a large Army order for bombers, he began to look about for a new location. Instead of looking for the city that would offer the most inducements Martin took his time and conducted a complete survey of the entire country with respect to transportation, labor, supplies, and waterways. He eliminated all but two possibilities: Atlanta, Georgia, and Baltimore, Maryland. From these he finally selected Baltimore. It had the seacoast, a good labor pool, the right location, and, in short, filled the bill in every particular.

Baltimore at that time was promoting Lindbergh Field, a development the city intended to make into a model ultramodern airport. The city was afire with the idea of bringing the Glenn L. Martin Company to Baltimore, and negotiations began with the city officials for a factory site right on the airport, in a deal that would give Martin the airport location at an attractive figure. For months, conference after conference was held, each time stopping short of settlement. Newspapers followed the course of the negotiations closely. Some began to take sides as politics seeped in, with the result that the whole thing became a political issue. Eventually, a rental proposition was offered to Martin. Preferring to own his factory outright he declined.

Meanwhile Martin realized that a satisfactory settlement was impossible. At the same time he knew that if he looked elsewhere around Baltimore values would immediately be boosted to prohibitive prices. Yet he had decided that Baltimore was his logical location, and he was determined to build there.

Glenn Martin is deceptively mild in appearance, with a quiet soft-spoken manner that seems to border on the naive. Many persons have imagined, in dealing with Martin, that he presented an easy target for manipulation, and quite a few have acted on that premise. Invariably such persons have been chagrined to discover that the innocuous, country-boy façade is just that, and that Glenn L. Martin has an odd trick of coming out on top.

He was in no great hurry on the Baltimore negotiations, for the Cleveland plant was still finishing up the last of his Army contract. Even after he had decided that political juggling in his airport negotiations was intolerable he continued to hold meetings and conferences. Meanwhile, however, he called in a purchasing agent and spreading out a map of the Baltimore area he put his finger on a spot. "Buy me this," he said, and while his agent in complete secrecy went about accumulating the fifty-odd parcels of land that made up the tract he went on with his hopeless negotiations.

When the last deed was signed he blandly announced his move to a spot eleven miles outside of Baltimore. His first unit there consisted of 1240 acres, ideally located for aircraft manufacture. It was on the Pennsylvania Railroad, at the water's edge, near to Baltimore's labor supply, and with room for expansion. Meanwhile, Lindbergh Field remained no more than a glimmering hope in the minds of its promoters.

One of the last of the pioneer fliers to maintain a leading role in the development of later aviation, Martin at his new location was ready to accept the challenge of Pan American Airways' demand for a transoceanic flying boat in 1931. After the new China Clippers had been put in service in 1935 Martin predicted that even bigger flying boats would be built before long. Said he in 1938, "As far as weight distribution and ability to fly are concerned, flying boats of 125 tons are perfectly feasible, according to our preliminary drafts." And so, by World War II, the giant "Mars" flying boat, world's largest, was seeing wartime military transport service in the Pacific.

That this new accomplishment was not startling to Martin can be seen in his remarks on the status of airplane manufacture made as early as 1938. "Aircraft manufacture has definitely emerged from the stage in which it was a spotty pioneering experiment," he said. "In the old days we went up only in perfect flying weather. Gradually, as planes improved, we learned to fly in all weather. And the field for improvement has been opened wider and wider by the development of new metals and alloys as well as by the constant experiments of the builders. Aircraft manufacture is now a real business."

The test of that "real business" came shortly, with the beginning of the Second World War. Then thousands of planes and engines of all types were manufactured in a supreme burst of speed . . . but that is another tale and does not belong in this story of aviation pioneers, except to show how aviation owes to their efforts its vigorous start, its early rise, and to illustrate that without the enterprise and ingenuity, the skill and perseverance of these early men, the later achievements could not have been accomplished so swiftly or so well.

Collaborator's Note

The sincere desire of the author to keep this book an impersonal record of the men it concerns has eliminated reference to the part played by Maurice Holland in many of the historic events mentioned.

However, it may interest the reader to know that Lieutenant Holland served in the Aviation Section of the Signal Enlisted Reserve Corps from July 30, 1917, until his honorable discharge on September 30, 1920, as the attached Army record shows. He worked with many of the men whose stories our book tells. He studied aeronautical engineering at Massachusetts Institute of Technology under Alexander Klemin and was assigned to Wright Field at Dayton when that was the center of testing for the Department of Military Aeronautics. "Shorty" Schroeder, later famous for his altitude records and other daring exploits, was then Chief Test Pilot and Lieutenant Holland was Assistant to the Chief of Aircraft Engines, Major Hallet, the same Major Hallet who was the engine expert on the projected Rodman Wanamaker flight referred to in the chapter on Erik Nelson.

When the Bureau of Military Aeronautics at Wright Field was combined with the Bureau of Aircraft Production at McCook Field, Lieutenant Holland was assigned as

Officer in Charge of Planes and Engine Maintenance—the same job in which Erik Nelson, Round-the-World flier, followed Holland. He has been associated with such well-known test pilots as Jimmy Doolittle, Leigh Wade (of the Round-the-World flight), H. R. Harris (who became the first member of the Caterpillar Club), C. C. Mosely, Casey Jones, and a number of others.

The experiments of Major Hoffman in developing the parachute, the night-flying experiments of Lieutenant Bruner, the engine developments of Lawrance, and other McCook Field achievements were all being made under the direct observation of Lieutenant Holland during his assignment at McCook.

Later he was Assistant Chief of Flying Section and was associated with such epoch-making events as the preparation of the Gordon Bennett racing plane which Major Schroeder took to France. He assisted in the engineering preparations for a number of important aviation exploits and participated in the First International Airplane Race from Toronto to New York and return in 1920. In this race he and Staff Sergeant Coombs were awarded gold wrist watches for the fastest time from Toronto to New York.

Still later, in an Air Service Demonstration, he and Coombs carried the pictures of the Willard-Dempsey heavyweight championship fight on the then longest cross-country flight at night, from Erie, Pennsylvania, to Mineola, Long Island, for which he was commended by the Director of Air Service.

In London in 1924, while attending the First World Power Conference as delegate on the part of the United States, he had the thrill of being present when the Army Round-the-World fliers landed at Croyden. There he enjoyed the opportunity to taxi the "New Orleans" to its hangar.

Mr. Holland continued his interest in aviation as a member of the first Committee on Commercial Aviation of the American Engineering Council, as one of the early members of the Advisory Committee of the Guggenheim School of Aeronautics of New York University, and has written on various aviation and industrial research subjects.

The statement of his military service follows:

WAR DEPARTMENT
The Adjutant General's Office
Washington, D. C.

The records of this office show that Maurice Holland enlisted on July 30, 1917, at Cambridge, Massachusetts, for the Aviation Section, Signal Enlisted Reserve Corps; reported for active duty on September 10, 1917; was ordered to duty with Detachment, Signal Enlisted Reserve Corps, Toronto, Canada, to undergo a course of instruction to qualify as pilot; was transferred on November 7, 1917, to Taliaferro Field, Fort Worth, Texas, and was honorably discharged, a private first class, on February 12, 1918, to accept a commission. He accepted commission as second lieutenant, Aviation Section, Signal Enlisted Reserve Corps, and was placed on active duty February 13, 1918, at Taliaferro Field, Fort Worth, Texas, he being required to participate regularly and frequently in aerial flights from that date. On February 22, 1918, he was ordered to duty with the

184th Aero Squadron, Fort Worth, Texas, where he was assigned as flying officer March 13, 1918, and was relieved May 16, 1918, to attend the School of Military Aeronautics at Cambridge, Massachusetts. On August 2, 1918, he was assigned to Wilbur Wright Field, Dayton, Ohio; on January 6, 1919, he was transferred to McCook Field, Dayton, Ohio, which remained his station until the date of his honorable discharge September 30, 1920.

The records show further that Lieutenant Holland was on special duty at various periods during his service and on July 8, 1919, he was commended by the Director of Air Service for intense interest in his work, devotion to duty, and the initiative and enthusiasm shown in connection with the assignment to take the pictures of the Willard-Dempsey fight from Erie, Pennsylvania, to New York.

INDEX

INDEX

INDEX

INDEX

North Island, training at, 28, 29

OX and OXX engines, 140, 141, 151, 152, 169
Ovington, Earle, 10

Pacific Ocean flights, 44, 184-86
Pacific Zeppelin Transport Company, 24
Packard Motor Company, 128, 135
Page, Handley, 13, 21, 200
Pan American Airways Corporation, 41, 44, 157-58, 175-77, 179-91
parachutes, 26, 39, 40, 113-26
parts of a plane, 37
Patrick, Major General Mason M., 123, 124
"Paul Revere's Horse," 161-62
Peabody, C. H., 10, 83-84
"Penguin," 168
Pershing, General John J., 35
Philippine Clipper, 186
photography, aerial, 26, 94-112, 139
pioneer aviators, 4-5
polar flights, Russian, 53
Potter, Colonel William, 31
Pratt & Whitney Aircraft Company, and Wasp, 40, 171
pressure, wind. *see* wind pressure
Priester, Andre, 180, 188
promoters, 37
propellers, blade element theory, 12
Puerto Rico, flight to, 54
Pulitzer Cup, 20

races, 20-22, 206
radio for planes, 8, 23, 187
Read, Commander A. C., 18
record flight system, 154
research, 4-6, 7-8, 14, 21-23, 38-39, 42-43
see also Massachusetts Institute of Technology
Resistance of the Air and Aviation, by Eiffel, 4, 7, 9-11
Rittenhouse, David, 21-22
round-the-world flight, Army Air Service (1924), 22, 39, 45-47, 54-60, 137
Royal Aeronautical Society (British), 8, 19
Russian polar flights, 53
Ryan monoplane, Lindbergh's, 162

safety competition, Guggenheim, 90-91
sand-testing, 86-87
Schneider Cup, 20-22

School of Aeronautics, Guggenheim, 80, 90, 92
schools, establishment of, 91
Schroeder, Major Rudolph, 66, 206, 207
scouting, air, 27, 28
searchlight, rotating, 76-77
Shenandoah, and loss of, 8, 19, 22, 25
Sikorsky S-4, 186
Simplified Aerodynamics, by Klemin, 91
Sims, Admiral William S., 19
Smith, Floyd, 117-18, 121
Smithsonian Institution, 11, 13-14
Sperry, Lawrence and plane, 169
"Spirit of Saint Louis," 162
Squantum meet, 10
Squier, General George O., 13
Standards, Bureau of, 12-13
Stevens, Albert W., 26, 39, 94-112
Stout, William B., and companies, 127-44
stratosphere flight, 110
Streett, St. Clair, 52, 54, 125
strength, plane. *see* stress analysis
stress analysis, work of Klemin, 86
stresses, wind. *see* wind pressure
struts, wing, 4
submarine, air protection against, 17

Taube, 14
Taylor, Admiral David W., 17, 18
technology. *see* research
Teddington, England, research at, 13
test flights, early, 88
testing, sand, 86-87
Towers, Lieutenant John, 17, 18
training, pilot, 29, 188
transAtlantic flight, first, 8, 18-19, 22, 44
transport, commercial. *see* commercial air transport
Trippe, Juan Terry, 175-91
tunnels, wind. *see* wind tunnels

United Airlines, 143

velocity, wind. *see* wind pressure
Vincent, Colonel Jesse, 31, 136
Vought plane, 21

Walcott, Charles D., 11
Wars, World. *see* World War I and II
Wasp, Pratt & Whitney, 40, 171
water-cooled engines. *see* engines
weather service, 22-23, 91
Whirlwind engine. *see* engines

213

INDEX